THERE'S A BABY IN THE HOUSE!

PREPARING YOUR DOG FOR THE ARRIVAL OF YOUR CHILD

MIKE WOMBACHER

Cover photos: Rose Guilbert
Cover design: Rebecca Johnson

ISBN 0-9713033-0-4

To contact Mike Wombacher:
Website: www.doggonegood.org
415.437.0848

TABLE OF CONTENTS

Acknowledgments 5
About the Author 6
Foreword 7

Introduction 9

Early Considerations 12
A Heads Up! 12

The Doggie Twelve-Step Program 17
Learn to Earn 17
Control Feeding Arrangements 19
Control Sleeping and Resting Areas 20
Make Your Dog Move Out Of Your Way 23
Control Access to Narrow Openings.. 24
Do Not Let Your Dog Pull Ahead of You on
the Lead 27
Do Not Let Your Dog Jump up on You As a Form of Greeting 31
Do Not Let Your Dog Take Food Without Your Permission 35
Control the Games Your Dog Is Allowed to Play 41
Do Not Let Your Dog Take Positions Above You 44
Groom and Handle Your Dog Regularly 46
Teach and Practice Obedience Exercises 48
A Springboard to the Future 49
Summary of the Doggie Twelve-Step Program 50

Addressing and Resolving Potential Behavior Problems 51
What if my dog doesn't like children? 52
What if my dog is afraid of, or aggressive towards, sudden
movements, loud noises, or any disruption of his immediate
environment? 58
What if my dog is sensitive and reactive to being touched
in certain ways? 60
What if my dog is emotionally dependent and afraid of
being left alone? 64
What if my dog is possessive over toys or food? 73
What if my dog barks excessively? 81
What if my dog is overly protective? 87
What if I have several dogs and they don't get along well together? 89
What if my dog has killed or seriously injured domestic animals 91

Dealing with the Serious Problem Dog 92

A Seamless Transition **95**

    Dogs, Children, and Toys 96
    The Child's Room and other Zones 97
    The Stroller 103
    A Little Theater 104
    Getting Closer 105
    The Moment of Truth 107

Looking into the Future **112**

A Few Final Thoughts **117**

Appendix **119**

Acknowledgments

There are so many people without whose help this book never would have come into existence that naming them all could, in itself, fill an entire volume. However, there are a few that deserve special mention for the exceptional contributions that they have made not only to this book but to my life as a whole.

First among these is my wife Rose who not only initially encouraged me to pursue my love of dog training as a career, but who relentlessly urged me on in writing this book. Next comes my good friend, Kirk Turner, dog trainer and human being extraordinaire, who years ago took me under his wing as an apprentice and helped kick start my professional life in the world of dogs. Then, of course, my parents, Klaus and Margot, as well as my sister Birgit who, throughout my tumultuous life, have never been anything but supportive and encouraging.

In terms of actually putting this book together, special thanks to Bruce Henderson for his exquisite illustrations, Rebecca Johnson for her wonderful layout work, once again my wife Rose for her photos, as well as the friends and clients who have contributed their photographs to help liven up these pages. Belinda Levinsen, Pam Raisin, Anne Marie Barnes, Katie Bracco, Candyce Plummer Gaudiani, Jane Reed, Kimberly Burke, Birgit Chasin, Sharon Miner and Bari Halperin — thanks bunches!

And finally, of course, a special thanks to all those clients who have allowed me to help them with their dogs thus providing me with the extensive real world experience that gave me the confidence to put this book together in the first place.

ABOUT THE AUTHOR

Michael Wombacher has been involved with dogs for over twenty years in a variety of capacities and since 1995 training and behavior modification have been his sole means of income. At this writing Mike has performed close to ten thousand in-home behavioral consultations covering the entire spectrum of dog behavior from the mundane to the bizarre. He has also taught classes, trained other trainers, helped run kennels as well as his own, small-scale boarding and training operation.

Mike has been certified as an expert on dog behavior by the California Superior Court and does occasional work evaluating dogs in legal matters. He has also been featured on the local news and has trained dogs for numerous celebrities.

His training approach focuses on channeling a dog's natural drives and instincts into behaviors acceptable in the human pack primarily through the principles of positive reinforcement and operant conditioning as well as through methods that appeal to the dog's canine sensibilities.

His training methods are so effective and his style so clear that Michael Tilson Thomas, music director of the San Francisco Symphony, and one of the great classical musicians of our time, commented that "Michael Wombacher is a maestro of dog trainers. His clarity of thinking, sense of humor, and skills in communicating make dog training fun for both pet and pet lover."

FOREWORD

There are a lot of dog training books on the market today and the information contained in these books is vast and confusing. So many different approaches and philosophies. It can boggle your mind. How do you choose?

If you are a novice at training dogs and do not have a good understanding of *all* these techniques and how to apply them to individual dogs, you may make some critical mistakes by mixing styles with your dog. Many of these books touch on individual issues only lightly, not going into much depth about anything and seem to me to be merely an affirmation of the writer's long career in showing dogs at obedience trials. Moreover, what is written does not necessarily correspond to all the techniques the authors have used with the dogs they compete with. Now, don't get me wrong! Showing in obedience at an AKC or mixed breed organization event is a worthwhile and rewarding hobby and I encourage everyone to pursue that hobby as it can teach a great deal about behavior and training.

However, Mike Wombacher has literally worked "in the trenches" around the San Francisco Bay Area for years helping busy families with their dogs. Real situations, real problems, hectic lifestyles. You name it, Mike has seen it. From dogs who have bitten people to ones who were so timid they wouldn't come out from under the bed. Most dog training books are not designed to help average families deal with these kinds of problems. And as Mike has alluded to in the title and text of this book, one of the biggest problems concerns the introduction of a baby into your household (read "pack").

This book is, in my opinion, a well balanced approach based on solid training principles that have been tested in Mike's program as well as my own and probably hundreds of other trainers who deal with the real world problems of average owners.

I was Mike's first human dog training teacher. He has worked with other trainers, doggy day care owners, and thousands of dogs and their families. He KNOWS how precious the dog/human relationship is and works daily to share his knowledge and develop that relationship with people and their pets.

The sections in this book are designed to provide a comprehensive program for basic relationship training plus great methods for introducing your new baby to the fold. The highlighted sections on the sides will give you quick reference to individual points while the body of the text goes to the heart of the matter.

Knowledge is power! Get ready to gain some valuable insights into the world of a professional dog trainer who knows his stuff. You can benefit from this program. Please read this book a couple of times and then refer to it often. If your dog has special or unusual issues, do not hesitate to call a behaviorist who displays an obvious affinity to dogs and people. For Mike and myself, our primary rule is: Do no harm to the dog!

Kirk Turner
Head Trainer, Owner
E-Z Train Dog Training
June, 2001

I was Mike's first human dog training teacher. He has worked with other trainers, doggy day care owners, and thousands of dogs and their families. He KNOWS how precious the dog/human relationship is and works daily to share his knowledge and develop that relationship with people and their pets.

The sections in this book are designed to provide a comprehensive program for basic relationship training plus great methods for introducing your new baby to the fold. The highlighted sections on the sides will give you quick reference to individual points while the body of the text goes to the heart of the matter.

Knowledge is power! Get ready to gain some valuable insights into the world of a professional dog trainer who knows his stuff. You can benefit from this program. Please read this book a couple of times and then refer to it often. If your dog has special or unusual issues, do not hesitate to call a behaviorist who displays an obvious affinity to dogs and people. For Mike and myself, our primary rule is: Do no harm to the dog!

Kirk Turner
Head Trainer, Owner
E-Z Train Dog Training
June, 2001

FOREWORD

There are a lot of dog training books on the market today and the information contained in these books is vast and confusing. So many different approaches and philosophies. It can boggle your mind. How do you choose?

If you are a novice at training dogs and do not have a good understanding of *all* these techniques and how to apply them to individual dogs, you may make some critical mistakes by mixing styles with your dog. Many of these books touch on individual issues only lightly, not going into much depth about anything and seem to me to be merely an affirmation of the writer's long career in showing dogs at obedience trials. Moreover, what is written does not necessarily correspond to all the techniques the authors have used with the dogs they compete with. Now, don't get me wrong! Showing in obedience at an AKC or mixed breed organization event is a worthwhile and rewarding hobby and I encourage everyone to pursue that hobby as it can teach a great deal about behavior and training.

However, Mike Wombacher has literally worked "in the trenches" around the San Francisco Bay Area for years helping busy families with their dogs. Real situations, real problems, hectic lifestyles. You name it, Mike has seen it. From dogs who have bitten people to ones who were so timid they wouldn't come out from under the bed. Most dog training books are not designed to help average families deal with these kinds of problems. And as Mike has alluded to in the title and text of this book, one of the biggest problems concerns the introduction of a baby into your household (read "pack").

This book is, in my opinion, a well balanced approach based on solid training principles that have been tested in Mike's program as well as my own and probably hundreds of other trainers who deal with the real world problems of average owners.

INTRODUCTION

 A few weeks before putting hand to keyboard to write this book I was sitting at my desk shaking my head in exasperation. I had just hung up with yet another couple who had decided to give up their dog three months after they had a child. "It's just too much," they told me in tears. "The dog pees every time we pay attention to our baby, he runs around the house and barks at her, growls when we put her on the sofa which he's no longer allowed on and seems to have generally gone crazy." When I told them what they would have to do to correct this situation they realized that with a new baby and two jobs they simply didn't have the time. Sadly they gave up the dog. What was really sad was that the whole situation was entirely preventable had they started working with their dog from the day they knew they were expecting.

At least twice a month I counsel expecting parents on how to prepare their dogs for the arrival of a child and after receiving this phone call I decided that the time had come to do put everything relevant to this subject down on paper. If more people had ready access to this information, I thought, perhaps less dogs would be re-homed within a few months of the baby's arrival. At any rate, with that motivation I set out to write this book. In it I have tried to cover every conceivable issue that could be related to bringing a child into a home with one or more dogs in it. From a great deal of practical experience I know that the things outlined in this book work. The biggest trick is getting people to do them – and sooner, rather than later. After all, like the clients mentioned above, soon you'll have a baby and precious little time for your dog. So, as they say, there's no time like the present. That having been said, let's take a quick look at how this book is organized and how it can help you.

In the first section, you will find information designed to help assess whether your relationship with your dog is healthy and conducive to the introduction of a new "pack member." If you find that it isn't, it will help you do what you have to to get it there. Additionally, it not only discusses ways to deal with a multitude of annoying canine antics but also *lays the groundwork* for the resolution of a variety of serious behavior problems. Because of its comprehensive nature I recommend that everyone read it in its entirety or at least thoroughly peruse this section as it contains all the fundamental building blocks of a wholesome relationship between you, your dog, and your new child.

In the second section, I address a variety of behavior problems that could make introducing a child into a dog's life problematic. You may search through this section to locate a discussion of problems you are experiencing. I'm sure you will find answers here. But first things first, *please keep in mind that reading the first section is foundational to any approaches to behavior modification outlined in the second.*

In the third section, I outline a series of pragmatic exercises designed to prepare your dog for the changes in your household that the arrival of your child will most certainly entail. I recommend that you read this section in its entirety and incorporate as many of the exercises as feasible into your life. They are designed to prepare your dog for all these changes and to teach him to build powerful positive associations with them. By preparing your dog for your baby's arrival, the day of the birth and all the upheaval that this will entail will be a mere bump in the road for him and everyone will live happily ever after.

Finally, a couple of notes on writing style. First, there are occasions throughout this book where I repeat myself. The reason for this is twofold. That is, some things bear repeating simply for emphasis but I also understand that certain readers may just skip around this book looking for answers to particular problems and I want to be sure that the points that are repeated are likely to be read by all. Second, there is the issue of gender. Throughout what follows I refer to both dogs and owners as "he." I assure you, this is not due to any gender bias on my part but simply due to limitations in the English language. Since we have no gender neutral personal pronouns available to us I have chosen to uniformly refer to everyone as "he" for the simple reason that I am a "he" and it's the most comfortable for me. I hope the reader understands and takes no offense. With that behind us let's dive in and see how we can prepare your dog for the arrival of your child.

Congratulations! You're pregnant and your "pack" will soon be growing. If you're like most people, you're caught between anticipation and trepidation. You're thrilled about the arrival of your new child and you're concerned about doing everything right. If you own a dog, certainly some of your concern revolves around him. You're probably asking yourself: "How will my dog handle this? Will he be jealous? Will he be careful?" And most importantly: "Is there any chance that he might bite my child?" If you're not concerned, you should be. Approximately 80% of dog bites happen to children under five. The purpose of this book is to help you find your way through these concerns, answer important questions, and set the stage for a warm and mutually beneficial relationship between your dog and your new child. In addition, this book will address the very difficult question of whether or not having the dog you have right now will be appropriate when your new child arrives.

Congratulations!

A HEADS UP!

Before discussing ways to ensure a smooth transition into siblinghood for your dog, it would be wise to assess whether there are any obvious potential problems looming on the horizon. On the following page I will provide a laundry list of questions you should ask yourself even if you're not pregnant but are simply considering the possibility. Take some time to observe your dog and answer these questions honestly. Doing so will raise any red flags and give you a head start in resolving any problems if they do indeed exist. If you find that no behavior problems exist, well, you're in good shape aren't you? Okay, here goes.

❖ Does my dog like children?

❖ Has he been exposed to them on a consistent basis?
  • If not, why not? If it's simply for lack of opportunity, then now would be a good time to start exposing him to children while you closely observe his responses.
    – Is he shy and intimidated?
    – Is he suspicious?
    – Is he overly exuberant and pushy?

❖ What is your dog's general disposition?
  • Is he sensitive to or fearful of novel stimulation such as loud noises, sudden movements, and rough handling?
  • Is he hand shy?
  • Is he emotionally dependent on you and generally spoiled?
  • Is he afraid of being left alone?
  • Is he pushy and demanding?

❖ Does your dog exhibit problematic behaviors?
  For example,
  • Does he bark at you for attention?
  • Does he jump up on you and your guests as a form of greeting?
  • Does he steal food from tables or beg incessantly at dinner time?
  • How does your dog relate generally to food and objects of possession?
    — Does he need his own area in which to eat or chew on his favorite toys?
    — Can you take anything away from him at any time without the slightest form of resistance?
      • If your dog does offer resistance what kind is it?
        – Does he simply tense up and look at you out of the corner of his eyes?
        – Does he growl?
        – Does he actually snap and bite?

- If your dog has furniture rights do you have trouble removing him from the furniture?
- Do you have trouble getting him to move out of your way if he's resting somewhere?
- Is your dog overly territorial?
- Does he threaten your guests?
- Does he bark excessively?
- Does your dog understand obedience commands?
  — If so, how well does he obey them?

If you have more than one dog in your household you should ask yourself the above questions about each dog and consider a few more:

❖ How do your dogs get along together?

❖ Do they ever fight?
- If so, over what?
  — Over food?
  — Over toys?
  — Over special places?
  — Over you?
  — Have they ever injured each other?

❖ Do they compete for your attention?

❖ Is it clear who is the dominant dog in your pack?

❖ Are you the dominant dog in your pack?

This latter issue is of utmost importance. Dogs are pack animals and by their very nature *crave* structure and authority or, in short, leadership. (By the way, this is true of children also). If a dog does not perceive leadership in his environment he will assume that the role, by default, is his. As political scientists will tell you: power, like nature, abhors a vacuum. A dog that perceives himself as leader in his human environment can be the source of a great deal of problems including many of those implied by the questions above. If you're planning to bring a child into a household in which your dog thinks he is the leader, whatever problems you are having now are highly likely to increase. Since introducing a baby will change the pack structure, your dog may feel the need to assert himself over any new members and reevaluate his relationship with existing members. Clearly, you don't want your dog asserting himself over your new baby. Even if your dog is not the assertive type and is more on the fearful side, the perception of a lack of effective leadership will often make such a dog even more fearful and can contribute to a behavioral disposition commonly known as fear-aggression. Thus, effective leadership is the foundation of the resolution not only of the behavior problems alluded to above but the seamless introduction of a new child to your pack.

Therefore, I'm going to begin by outlining what I refer to as my *Doggie Twelve-Step Program*. This is a rank management program designed to put you in charge and forms a springboard for discussing the resolution of any potential problems. Even if you don't feel that you're experiencing any problems with your dog, the application of this program may reveal areas of difficulty that you were not aware of. Moreover, a great many elements of this routine should be implemented even if you're having no trouble with your dog simply because they assure good and safe behavior in all situations, especially those including children. As you read through this program you may find that some of the things discussed

What is leadership?

*Being your dog's leader does not mean being a bully. True leadership has to do with confidence, the ability to give direction, and the willingness to follow through on directions given. It also has to do with being trustworthy and reasonable in the demands one makes. A great general does not lead because he can beat up his soldiers. He leads because he embodies certain qualities that make others want to take that lead. Embodying leadership qualities will make your dog look to your for direction more than any act of brute force ever could. And lest you should be concerned that your dog will no longer like you if you take charge of his life, please be assured that the person who puts the most pressure on a dog **in a fair way**, gets the lion's share of that dog's love, affection and respect.*

apply directly to your situation and others don't. Feel free to implement what makes sense in your context and don't worry about what doesn't. If you find that your dog is perfectly well-mannered in relation to all the things outlined below, consider yourself lucky and, by all means, move along through the rest of this book.

LEARN TO EARN

If a dog believes that everything is coming to him simply because he exists it will be easy for him to become, well, a "legend in his own mind." In a pack situation the leader dog basically gets anything he wants anytime he wants from anyone he wants. This is in keeping with his position and makes perfect sense in that context. If in the human context the same thing happens, that is, the dog basically gets whatever he wants without any demands being placed on him he simply has no choice but to draw the conclusion that he must be in charge. After all, if he weren't why would everyone be so compliant? It follows that since he views himself as being in charge he would also view himself as having a variety of rights, rights that could lead him to act in inappropriate ways. Therefore the first step in adjusting the dog's view of himself is to make him earn a living. What that means is that for every nice thing you do for your dog he must do something for you first. For example, before you give him so much as a pat on the head you should ask him for an obedience command, even if it's something as simple as "sit." If he doesn't do it, you gently but firmly and quickly make him. Any other nice things you do for him such as feeding him, taking him for a walk, or playing with him should be preceded by some type of demand. And be sure that it's not always the same demand. In other words, don't just always ask him for a sit. Be sure to ask him for downs, for stands, for a short bit of heeling, or even something silly like a trick. It doesn't really matter what it is so long as he's doing something for you before you do something for him. Always asking him for the same thing is referred to as "pattern training" and defeats the purpose of what you're trying to accomplish. That is, if the dog is pattern trained, he's really only running off his own internal mechanism and not truly looking to you for direction, which is precisely the habit you want to get him into. In short, *He should get used to looking to you for direction in all things* that are important to him. This will begin to position you as leader in

A legend in his own mind.

your dog's mind. For most dogs this little routine goes a long way to ensuring a proper attitude towards their owners. However, some dogs aren't quite that easy.

If you're experiencing serious attitude problems with your dog (if he's the pushy and demanding type), it's also useful to spend some time during the day actively ignoring him. In other words, during a period of time that he is used to having your attention simply cold-shoulder him. This means *do not look at, speak to, or touch him.* If he comes over to pester you for attention either get up and walk off, run him through a bunch of obedience drills or simply tell him to go away. If he is the super pushy type and refuses to go away, often a squirt from a water bottle (or, if water doesn't bother him try a taste deterrent such as Bitter Apple™ spray, or a breath spray like Binaca™) right on his nose and mouth should convince him to depart. For those pushy dogs used to demanding their owner's undivided attention most of the time, this kind of treatment will often come as a shock. In fact, they may even go through a short period of depression. This is perfectly normal and is actually a good sign. It means that the dog knows things are changing and the upset usually passes after three to seven days. The more spoiled the dog was the longer the period of depression typically lasts, but every dog invariably gets over it and then comes to terms with the new situation. From this the foundation of a whole new relationship can be built.

I have found that this part of the program—turning one's attention into a valued resource rather than having it taken for granted when dealing with a dog with an attitude problem—is often the most emotionally challenging part for the owner. But trust me, once you get through this your dog will love and respect you more, not less, than he did before and I promise that you will not break his spirit. On the contrary, you'll teach him how to live with you in an acceptable way, which will make your partnership more fulfilling for both of you.

Simply executing this part of the rank management program will cause your dog to perceive you in an entirely new way. He will immediately begin to respect you, and yes, love you more. Remember, dogs crave leadership and the fact is that *the person who puts the most pressure on a dog in a fair way gets the lion's share of the dog's love, affection and respect.*

CONTROL FEEDING ARRANGEMENTS

Food is the primary survival resource. Food is to dogs what money is to people. Therefore, whoever controls the food commands a great degree of respect and authority. As a general rule, among wolves, the more dominant individuals have access to the premium pieces of food and others have to wait their turn in accordance with their status. And so it goes down the line with the least dominant dogs usually having to settle for what is left over. This understanding is genetically programmed into your dog and you can take advantage of it in order to assert your leadership in a very non-confrontational way.

The following routine will allow you to send a very strong message to your dog about control of the food resource and therefore your authority.

Begin by preparing your dog's food in front of him in as enticing a way as possible. Go ahead, be theatrical. The goal is to get your dog as worked up over the food as possible in anticipation of a yummy meal. However, just when he thinks he's about to get his meal, take his dish and place it up on a counter were he cannot get it. Then go over, sit down at the table and have something to eat. Put the dog in a down-stay or tie him near you and proceed to eat. If the dog begins to pester you for the food by barking or whining, a quick squirt with the water bottle or Bitter Apple™ spray prefaced by a "quiet" command should do the trick. Let him know in no uncertain terms that he is not to bother you while you are eating. Take your time and enjoy your food. Try to build as

Step 2

Food is to dogs what money is to people.

much tension in the dog in relation to the food as possible. When you are completely finished with your meal, go back into the kitchen, take his food off the counter, show it to him and ask him to do a couple of obedience commands. Then go ahead and give it to him.

The point is that your dog should observe his food on the counter were he cannot get it. Then he should observe you going to eat and notice that he's not being allowed to participate. He cannot have his food or yours because you control both resources and, after all, pack leaders eat first. Only when you are good and ready is the dog allowed access to his food, and even that only happens after he has performed several obedience commands and therefore earned his meal. This significance of all of this in terms of rank is definitely not lost on your dog. Not only that, but this exercise also teaches him self-control around food, a discipline which will be a great asset once you have a child around.

Control Sleeping and Resting Areas

One of the ways a leader dog asserts himself is by controlling space with his body. He has the right to sleep or to rest anywhere he likes and to demand that other others move away from his favorite spots. He may also insist that if he is lying in a certain spot no one come within a few feet of him. This is what I call his "critical zone" and a dog tends to view this as an extension of himself. One clear sign that you have a problem with rank is if your dog growls, snaps, or even shows milder forms of resistance towards you when you approach or try to move him from his favorite places. In fact, this is one of the most common situations in which owners get bitten by their own dogs. If your dog has bitten or threatened to bite you in this context please read the section entitled *Dealing with the Serious Problem Dog* on page 92. An important aspect of sending the right message regarding rank to your dog is to control access to all furniture, beds, and favorite resting places. The benefits of such control when a youngster

Comfy, eh?

is around should be self-evident. There are a couple of ways you can approach this and which you choose is completely up to you. You can either choose to eliminate all furniture rights for your dog or you can choose to teach him that he's only allowed up with your invitation and that he must get off the moment you demand it. You can even teach him that he's only allowed on certain pieces of furniture, of course also dependent on your invitation. If you choose one of the latter I would recommend eliminating furniture rights altogether in the short term and using this as a default position. You can reintroduce furniture rights with your invitation once this is solidly understood.

Access to sleeping and resting areas may be controlled in a number of ways. You can reprimand your dog with a sharp "no" or "off" (use your squirt bottle or simply grab the dog in order to enforce this, if necessary) every time he begins to get up on a piece of furniture, close the doors to those areas where he likes to make himself at home, booby trap furniture items with sheets of tin foil, *upside down* mouse traps or scat mats (rubber mats emitting a static pulse), or simply keep the dog leashed to you in order to deny him access to these places. This last strategy is often very effective simply because

Photo: Rose Guilbert

Letting your dog drag a leash around is a great way to keep a handle on him.

its denies the dog any freedom of movement other than where you direct him, thus firmly putting you in a leadership position. Letting him drag a leash around the house—an extension of this—is another very effective way to control his movements. It allows you to simply pull him off the sofa or the bed by the end of the leash rather than having to grab for him.

If your dog has favorite places to sleep and you sense that he's attached to them to a fault (in other words, he might defend them) it's a good idea to deny him access to these places as well. *You don't want the dog having any sense of ownership over special places.* An easy way to deny him access to those places is by asking him to sleep in a different location each night. Tying him to a different spot every evening is a good way to accomplish this. Now don't get me wrong. The idea is not to make him uncomfortable, only to make him lose his sense of possession over favorite places. By all means make sure he's cozy. Just control where that takes place.

A Rental Agreement

Possession is nine tenths of the law, the old saying goes. Make sure you possess the rights to all furniture and resting places and if you do allow your dog access to these areas make sure it's on a "sublet" basis only.

Once the dog has relinquished furniture rights for some period of time and has resigned himself to this, you may, as stated above, reintroduce them on your terms *if you so desire.* There are a number of ways to do this. You can teach the dog to come up on an "invitation only" basis. The invitation can be a simple phrase such as "c'mon up," accompanied by a pat on the sofa. You can also do what I do. I have a special blanket that I lay on the sofa when I want my dog up with me. This keeps her from getting any dirt on the furniture and it's also a visual cue for permission to come up. When she sees the blanket come out she knows she's about to be invited up. I still say "c'mon up" and pat the blanket before she's allowed up just to be sure that she doesn't confuse that blanket with others (this is especially important with a baby around). By controlling the behavior in this way you can control access to your furniture while being able to snuggle with your dog on the sofa as well. In short, allow your dog access to the furniture on a "sublet" basis only and you can have your cake and eat it too.

Make Your Dog Move Out Of Your Way

Step 4

Another way to control space and assert your role as leader is to simply make your dog move out of your way as you are walking around home. As just mentioned, many pushy dogs like to control space with their bodies. This means that you often find them lying right in major thoroughfares in your house such as hallways, doorways and other areas that see a lot of traffic. Often, not wanting to bother the dog, you might find yourself simply walking around him, thinking that you should just let him have his space. This can be a mistake. It potentially sends him the signal that you are deferring to his authority by avoiding contact with him and respecting his "critical zone" when he's resting. What you should do instead, is to simply ask him to get up and move. Of course, if your dog is sleeping you should have the courtesy to wake him up first. The command I use to ask the dog to move out of my way is simply "excuse me." Approach your dog, clap your hands, and then, in a happy tone, say "excuse me." If the dog does not move out of your way relatively quickly you can gently nudge him with your foot to demand he move. You should look for multiple opportunities each day to ask the dog to move out of your way. Eventually, if you have used this exercise effectively, when your dog sees you coming he will simply get up and move without having to be asked. If your dog has bitten or threatened to bite you in this context please read the section entitled *Dealing with the Serious Problem Dog* on page 92.

Whose house is it anyway?

Step 5

CONTROL ACCESS TO NARROW OPENINGS

When you pass through a door or other narrow passageway, you should go first and your dog should wait to be asked to follow. This is not only an important exercise from a safety standpoint (you don't want your dog dragging you out the door when you've got a newborn on you), it has certain psychological implications as well. Part of the pack leader's job is to lead the pack into productive and new situations. If your dog is bolting through the doorway every time he sees a crack of light, he's taking charge. It's important to understand that for your dog the doorway represents a huge change of consciousness. From your perspective, the two of you are merely going for a walk but from your dog's perspective you're going hunting. In short, he's moving from the "den" to the "hunt." These two modes are about as far apart in his sensory experience as possible. Your dog's whole psychic and sensory awareness has gone from a state of being almost totally dormant to a state of extreme alertness and stimulation in a matter of a few moments. No wonder he's bouncing around at the front door. Keep in mind, for your dog there is nothing as pleasurable as "hunting"—this is about as primal as it gets. Therefore, he should understand that he needs to go through you to access that state of consciousness. You should become the doorway through which he must pass in order to have access to any of the things that are important to him, including the "hunt."

There are several very effective and easy ways to teach your dog not to pass the doorway before you. The first is to simply open the door just a hair as your dog is approaching it and when he makes a dash for it slam it in his face (not *on* his

That's a good boy.

Can you imagine a baby in this scenario?

Take Charge

Taking control of every aspect of your dog's life will cause him to have tremendous confidence in you. Not only that, it will allow you to safely integrate your dog into every aspect of your life thus making the relationship more fulfilling for both of you.

Want to go for a walk?

Not so fast!

face, please!). (See photos).
Timing is of the essence here.
You should avoid trapping the
dog's head in the door and
hurting him. The point is to
simply have the door slam
shut in front of his face, loudly
if possible, just a fraction of a
second before he gets there in
order to seriously startle him. As soon as he backs
off, open the door again just a hair. Usually the dog
will make a second run for it. If he does, you simply
repeat the procedure. Now he will be somewhat
cautious. You again open the door, this time a bit
further. If he makes another run for it you again
slam it in his face. Usually by this time the dog will
be confused. You continue to open the door ever
further and tempt your dog to run out and repeat
this procedure until he will not attempt to rush
the door. Usually there will be a moment where
the dog, in utter confusion, will look at you as if
to say, "Hey, what's going on here?" This is your
moment of opportunity. While he's looking at
you in confusion, ask him to sit. Very often you will find that
he will respond promptly. Confusion is a great place for

Photos: Rose Guilbert

That's better!

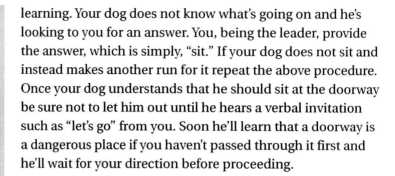

learning. Your dog does not know what's going on and he's looking to you for an answer. You, being the leader, provide the answer, which is simply, "sit." If your dog does not sit and instead makes another run for it repeat the above procedure. Once your dog understands that he should sit at the doorway be sure not to let him out until he hears a verbal invitation such as "let's go" from you. Soon he'll learn that a doorway is a dangerous place if you haven't passed through it first and he'll wait for your direction before proceeding.

Another, more direct way, to teach him the same concept is to simply attach his leash to his training collar. I prefer pinch collars which, despite their ferocious appearance, are actually the most humane training collars available, reducing the level of force you use on your dog by about 95% and almost completely eliminating any possibility of injuring him (see appendix). Open the door in the same way, and if he makes a run for it, give him a rather sharp correction just at the moment that his nose passes the threshold of the doorway. I feel justified in this situation giving the dog a rather sharp snap on the leash since the situation represents such a significant safety concern for you, your child, and your dog. I would like him to understand that passing through a doorway without permission is a dangerous undertaking, which indeed it is. If he tries it again, repeat the procedure. Again, once he inhibits himself ask him to "sit" and once he's settled tell him "let's go." Either one of the above procedures will teach your dog to look to you before passing through the doorway, but I prefer the first since it involves no real discomfort to the dog. With some dogs, the really headstrong type, using both techniques in succession is necessary to really make the exercise bulletproof.

Finally, if you want your dog really paying attention to you consistently, always ask him for a different command before permitting him to go out the door. In other words, instead of always asking him to sit, occasionally ask him to down, or to stand, or anything else you can think of. Never knowing what's coming next keeps him looking to you for direction which, of course, is the entire point.

DO NOT LET YOUR DOG PULL AHEAD OF YOU ON THE LEAD

Unless you're training for the Iditarod, your dog should never pull on his leash. He should learn to walk without ever putting any tension into the leash while also remaining oriented towards you. In far too many cases, from the point of view of the dog, the owner is merely piece of dead weight on the end of the leash to be dragged around. Trying to walk a dog like this, especially if there's a newborn in a stroller or a baby carrier, can be not only annoying, but also dangerous. Moreover, from the perspective of the dog, the idea he's getting should be obvious—he's leading the parade, not you. Definitely the wrong impression! Your dog needs to learn to walk on a loose lead while keeping at least half of one eyeball on you at all times. This does not mean that he has to walk alongside you in a formal heel position, but it does mean needs to pay attention to you. This reorientation of the dog is achieved through something I call the "Pay Attention Game."

Put your thumb through the leash handle.

Take up some slack.

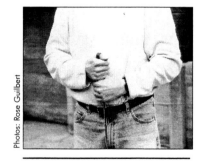

Drop and lock!

Photos: Rose Guilbert

Begin by putting a pinch collar (see the appendix for a discussion of pinch collars) on your dog. You must be sure that collar is on nice and snug. Loose pinch collars have a nasty tendency to fall off since part of what holds them together is a little tension between the links. Moreover, the looser the collar, the more firm a correction you need to deliver in order for the collar to have its action. Finally, if a pinch collar is too loose the prongs, instead of pinching slightly the way they're supposed to, can actually stab the dog in the neck, definitely an undesirable turn of events. Since the whole point of the pinch collar (no pun intended) is to take as much physical force as possible out of training, having it on loose would be entirely counterproductive.

Once the pinch collar is fit snugly, attach your six-foot leash to it. Then, as shown in the pictures to the left, insert your thumb through the leash handle and take up a little slack creating a loop in your hand (see photos this page). If the pinch collar is a new piece of equipment for your dog, the first thing you must do is to introduce it gently in order to let him know that there is something new happening on his neck today. Start your introductory exercise by simply walking with the dog. As you see that he is beginning to forge ahead and either *a)* pulling on the leash or *b)* simply failing to pay at least some attention to you, suddenly drop the slack in the lead, grab the leash handle with both hands like a baseball bat, hold it firmly near your belly button, and stop (see photos on opposite page). Since the dog is not paying attention, he will continue to walk and suddenly hit the end of the leash with the force of his own momentum. This will deliver a minor correction and usually cause the dog to turn around and look at you with a startled expression. At this point, encourage him to come back to you with a pat on your thigh and once he's near you again, praise him and resume your walk, being sure to take up the slack as you had before. Then, simply repeat the procedure. You will find that very soon your dog will begin to stay a little bit closer to you and pay a little bit more attention to what you're up to. Ultimately when you stop, your dog will automatically stop as well. This little exercise gently gets the dog used to the pinch collar and teaches him the fundamental concepts of the "Pay Attention Game," which are don't pull and keep an eye on me. Once this happens, you're ready for the next step.

Begin walking with the dog.

Begin by walking (see photos, next page) with your dog as you did a moment ago. Again, when you see that the dog is forging ahead it's time to take action. However, now when you drop the slack in the leash, instead of just stopping, you turn around and *without warning your dog* march briskly in the opposite direction. Again, the dog will hit the end of the leash, but this time not only will he hit it with the force of his own momentum, he will also feel your momentum going in the opposite direction. Most likely, if you followed the previous exercise, your dog will already have caught on to this trick and will know what to do to avoid a more noticeable correction. But if he hasn't, the correction he receives from this exercise will give him a very strong incentive to keep a close eye on you and follow you wherever you're going. Of course, once your dog is near you you should praise him wildly and thus teach him that being near you, paying attention is the "safe place" and being "out there" not paying attention is potentially where unpleasant things happen. Pretty soon, you'll find

When he forges or fails to pay attention, just stop. Do not yank!

Immediately encourage the dog to return to you and praise

Once again, begin walking with the dog

This time when your dog forges, drop the slack in the leash, as shown above, lock it into your bellybutton and briskly march in the opposite direction. Do not yank!

And, of course, enthusiatically praise as your dog catches up with you.

Photos: Rose Guilbert

that it's nearly impossible to lose your dog. When you've arrived at this point, start exposing him to increasingly distracting situations in order to test his willingness to pull on the leash.

In the correct performance of this exercise there are three points that are extremely important which I'll repeat simply for emphasis: *a)* drop the slack in the leash just *before* turning, *b)* don't issue any type of verbal warning to your dog (this would put all the pressure for alerting him to changes in direction on you rather than on him, where it should be), and *c)* make sure you *do not yank* him after he's made his turn. Once your dog learns to avoid the correction, you'll find that he'll walk near you without putting any tension in the leash and will also shadow your movements most of the time. In other words, you've now become relevant and he's following you, not dragging you down the street. In this context, it doesn't really matter whether the dog is walking slightly ahead of you, slightly behind you or a little out to the side. *What matters is that he's paying attention to you.* In other words, if when the dog is out ahead of you and you drop your slack and turn in the opposite direction, he is right with you, then who is the leader? Clearly you are! In short, your walk with him is now not only much safer and more pleasurable, it becomes yet another opportunity for you to assert your leadership role.

DO NOT LET YOUR DOG JUMP UP ON YOU AS A FORM OF GREETING

Jumping up, while usually a friendly gesture of greeting, is not only pushy and dominant, it also presents obvious problems when you are trying to navigate through your day with a small child in tow. Your dog should learn that the fastest way for him to get your attention and affection when greeting you is to keep all four feet on the ground. This can be accomplished very simply. As shown in the photos on the following page, take a squirt bottle, one that will allow you to shoot a jet stream, fill it with water and *hide it behind your back* so that the dog cannot see it. Then, enter the area where your dog would be likely to jump up on you and give him a quick squirt right on the nose and mouth while loudly saying "off" (more on this command in a moment). *Then, just as fast, return the bottle to its hiding place behind your back.* This will often come as a great shock to him. As he's recovering from his shock, actually encourage him to jump up on you again by speaking to him in a sweet voice, patting your chest and doing basically anything that will tempt him to repeat this maneuver. In human terms, this is called "entrapment" and it might seem inherently unfair. However, in training terms it is called a "set up" and is wonderfully useful. In this case, the point is to set him up and then teach him that no matter what it looks like, there is simply no reason for him to jump up. Children habitually do all sorts of things that tempt dogs to jump on them, yet your dog should learn to restrain himself regardless lest he inadvertently injure your child. If you find that water is simply too innocuous for your dog, you can fill the squirt bottle with Bitter Apple™ spray, a taste deterrent commonly available at pet shops. Binaca™, the breath spray, will also work quite well

Too much of a good thing.

Practice this exercise diligently both in relation to your guests (squirt him when he jumps on them) and yourself and soon you'll notice that your dog will begin to control himself. Now, do not overlook this very positive development! Too many

Be sure to conceal the
squirt bottle behind your
back.

Not so fast.

Photos: Rose Guilbert

That's better.

dogs only get attention when they're acting out in ways that are annoying while good behavior hardly gets a second look. In other words, once you see that your dog is restraining himself you should find a way to *reinforce the opposite behavior*, that is, not jumping up. In fact, the second he makes the decision not to jump on you, or perhaps even sit, bend down and reward him with attention, praise and perhaps even a handy and well-timed treat. In this way, he learns that all the praise, attention and affection that he is looking for will come to him automatically if he simply keeps four feet on the ground. It also teaches him to maintain a certain degree of social distance, even in highly charged situations, another form of respect for you.

If your dog happens to jump up on you when you don't have a squirt bottle handy, there are a number of other maneuvers with which you may surprise him. For example, if he jumps up on you, grab both his feet, one firmly in each hand, and hold them away from your body as if you were dancing with him. While you're doing this apply some firm pressure to his paws while simultaneously walking him backwards. This will likely make him very uncomfortable and he'll struggle to get away from you. Continue to hold him for a few moments while he's struggling and then finally release him. He'll soon catch on.

Another method involves simply grabbing your dog's muzzle, squeezing it shut as he jumps up you, and then gently but firmly pushing him into a sitting position on the ground. Similarly, rather than grabbing the muzzle you can use your hands to quickly bop him on his chest, sort of shoving him back towards the ground, and then immediately guide him into a sit. In either case, the moment he's sitting begin petting and praising him.

Finally, if he's on a leash, you can lower it so that some of it is on the ground and then stand on that section. This way, every

A Canine Handshake

Your dog jumping up on people is the canine equivalent of you going up to a perfect stranger, wildly throwing your arms around him and giving him a kiss as a form of greeting. While friendly and well intentioned, such a greeting would be totally inappropriate and would most likely get you beaten up or arrested. A handshake is what's called for and the canine equivalent of a handshake is a sit-stay.

time your dog begins to jump up he'll get about three inches off the ground and hit the end of the leash, a built-in, perfectly timed correction. This will almost always automatically guide him back to a sitting position where you can tell him what a good boy he is.

Whichever approach you use, be sure to be consistent and diligent and soon you'll find that your jumping problem will evaporate into the mists of distant memory.

Photo: Rose Guilbert

Standing on the leash is simple and efficient.

Do Not Let Your Dog Take Food Without Your Permission

As you saw earlier, food is the primary survival resource and control of the food resource is highly symbolic and meaningful to the dog. Too many dogs are way too pushy around food, sometimes going so far as to actually grab things out of people's hands. Clearly this is totally inappropriate and even dangerous if a small child is involved (if your dog has bitten or threatened to bite you in relation to food and objects please read the section entitled *Dealing with the Serious Problem Dog* on page 92.) Therefore one of the most important things to teach your dog is a very solid "off" command. To do this you need a handful of very yummy treats, and a squirt bottle filled with either water or Bitter Apple™ spray (what you use depends on your dog's sensitivity). Begin by holding a treat in front of him and saying "take it." Your dog should promptly come over and take the treat at which point you offer him another, saying "take it" again. Once more he'll come over and grab the treat. Repeat this procedure five or six times until your dog is really anticipating receiving a treat. Then suddenly, without warning, as he approaches the next treat, instead of saying "take it" command "off." If the dog

Keep your Paws to Yourself Please

If you allow your dog to take food from you without your permission it will be easy for him to conclude that he can do the same with your child. This, in turn, will teach him that your child is an easy mark for a food mugging and he will most likely conclude that junior is also a lower ranking pack member. Being a lower ranking pack member, your dog may conclude that he has the right to reprimand him, which he does not!

continues to go for the treat, which most likely he will since he does not know the "off" command, quickly spray him on the nose with whatever is in your squirt bottle. Usually the dog will back off with a shocked expression on his face. As soon as he does this you praise him enthusiastically and offer him the treat again with the suggestion to "take it". It might require a few repetitions for him to become totally confident in taking the treat once more but when he does, you repeat the procedure. You'll be amazed at how fast your dog will learn to understand that it's okay to take the treat with the "take it" command but that when he hears the "off" command he should immediately back off.

There are a couple of important points that need to be mentioned here. First, *your timing must be flawless*. That is, you must pause for a moment between issuing the "off" command and spraying the dog. This moment of time represents his window of opportunity. In other words, he needs to have a moment to process the command and comply. This allows him a chance to avoid the correction with the squirt bottle and this, of course, is the entire point. In this case, the word "off" becomes the cue that lets him know if he backs out of the situation immediately, nothing unpleasant will happen to him.

Second, it is important to be very sneaky with the bottle. In other words, you should not make it too obvious. Hiding it behind your back and bringing it out just as you're about to spray him is the best tactic. Then, as fast as it came out, the bottle should disappear again so that your dog has just a second or so of exposure to it. You want him to understand that the deterrent is the command "off," not the fact that you have a bottle. If the dog learns that the bottle is the deterrent he will forever be looking for it and, if he doesn't see it, may be tempted to continue with the behavior. You don't want him weighing and measuring. Instead, you want him to think that you potentially have that squirt bottle on you at all times. Once he believes that, he will stop testing you.

Continue with this exercise until you cannot get the dog to take the treat once the command "off" has been issued. When he has a solid understanding of this, then go to the next step by taking a treat and throwing it on the ground. Again, initially let him have three or four treats prefaced with the command "take it," and then at some point issue the "off" command once more. Again, if he does not immediately retreat he gets sprayed. Keep your timing in mind. Give him a moment to respond before you spray him. Once your dog has a solid understanding of these exercises then use the "off" command in various contexts around the house. For example, you can be standing in the kitchen working on dinner and suddenly throw a piece of food on the ground. When the dog goes to get it you command "off" as before and if he leaves it alone he's a good boy; if he doesn't he gets sprayed.

An Ally

A solid "off" command is one of your best allies in helping to teach your dog what is appropriate and what isn't as well as ensuring good manners around your child. Practice this often and in as many situations as possible.

Once your dog has learned this part of the exercise and is no longer taking food without your permission, you can move to the next level of the "off" command. Put him on his leash and pinch collar and take him outside. Also take along a handful of treats. While you are walking suddenly, and without warning, throw a treat on the street a few feet in front of him where he can see it. Once again, the first three to five times simply let him have it. Then suddenly command "off" as he begins to approach the treat. If your dog does not immediately turn away, give him a quick snap on the collar. Usually what will happen is that he will, with a very surprised look, turn his head towards you. The moment he does, give him a treat. *You do this even if you had to give him a correction.* Over time this teaches him that when you command "off" he should not only get off whatever he was focused on, but that he should look at you as well. You are now giving him two powerful motivators to take his eyes off whatever they're focused on. First, there is the threat of a correction that he has learned he can avoid by backing away from whatever he's interested in. Second, he is rewarded for giving you his attention once he hears the "off" command. That's about as black and white as you can make it. (See photos next page).

The "off" command. For the purpose of these pictures I used a bag rather than throwing a treat.

As the dog approaches I command "off" and if the dog doesn't comply, give a short snap.

When the slightly startled dog returns I offer a treat.

Photos: Rose Guilbert

Once he's learned the concept of "off" in a training context it's time to start using it in a variety of situations. Until your dog has thoroughly internalized this concept be sure to be prepared with your squirt bottle (hidden behind your back) so if he should test you, you can correct him. If you're very consistent with this for even a short period you'll soon find that you won't need that squirt bottle at all. In this context, also teach your dog that food on surfaces such as coffee tables and kitchen counters is off limits as well. Set tempting morsels out where the dog can see them and pretend not to watch. Of course, when the dog makes a move on the items you should explode with a very loud "off" and launch an assault with your squirt bottle.

Finally there's the "atomic off." This is the Ph.D. program of the "off" command. Take a plate of food, something really wonderful that your dog simply won't be able to resist, and place it in the middle of your living room floor. Then take him by the collar, walk him over to it, point to the item and tell him in a firm voice "off." Then walk him away to some other part of the room and let him go. Now, the idea is that since he's heard you say "off" in relation to the plate of food he shouldn't think of going near it. The reality is that that's probably not going to happen just yet. What's more likely is that shortly after you release your dog he'll find his way back to the food and attempt to go for it. Of course you or an accomplice will be lying in wait, hopefully in an area where it won't be so obvious to the dog. In one hand you should have a squirt bottle and in the other a shake can (an empty soda can with five or six pennies in it and a piece of tape across the top to keep them from falling out) and when your dog arrives near the food with his intent clear, you explode on him. Rattle your shake can, squirt him in the nose, scream bloody murder and chase him down the hall until he's running for his life. The idea is to scare the daylights out of him and convince him that going after something once you've told him "off" is an extremely dangerous undertaking. Once you've completed this reprimand you should leave the plate of food out for the rest of the night. If your dog makes another run for it he's telling you that you weren't sufficiently convincing the first time around so you need to ramp up the level of your reprimand. If you've done this properly your dog will not only avoid that plate of food for the rest of the night, he'll learn to take your "off" commands more seriously in the future.

Rights and Privileges

Paradoxically, imposing structure, constraints and certain limitations on your dog now will allow you to give him more freedom later. As he shows an increasing capacity to be responsible he may be allowed access to new freedoms in due course. Sound familiar? The same is true with kids.

Teaching your dog not to take food without your permission via a strong "off" command not only helps him understand your rank and authority, it is eminently practical as well, especially with a child on the way. Every household with young children I've ever visited is inherently chaotic. There are toys, food, and a variety of other items randomly strewn around all over the place. Having a strong "off" command in place will be extraordinarily useful in managing your dog and preventing him from getting into things which he shouldn't be into or which could be dangerous for him. In fact, without an effective "off" command you'll find yourself either endlessly and futilely screaming "no" at your dog or simply locking him up. In this context it's very easy for your dog to associate being locked up with the presence of your child, a scenario you want to avoid at all costs. Teaching a powerful "off" command opens numerous channels of communication with your dog and is fundamental to many of the exercises that will follow in subsequent sections of this book.

Paradoxically, having a strong "off" command also allows you to give your dog more freedom—in due course. For instance, once his "off" is bulletproof you may, if you like, feed him from the table. Most people are shocked when I tell them that I not only feed my dog from the table but that every dog trainer I know does so also. The reason you are able to do this without sending the wrong signals to your dog is because you're able to control all aspects of the behavior. For instance, if I don't want my dog near the table I simply tell her "off" and she leaves. If I do want to share some food with her I invite her over and either make her do a few cute tricks that I've taught her or simply have her hold a quiet down-stay at my feet. Either of these behaviors will be followed by tidbits from my plate. Now, I'm not suggesting that you should feed your dog from the table if you don't want to. I'm just offering another example of how, through good training, you can have your cake and eat it too.

CONTROL THE GAMES YOUR DOG IS ALLOWED TO PLAY

As you've already seen, a dog who has access to any resource he wants any time he wants can easily develop an attitude problem. Both toys and games are valuable resources and should therefore be controlled. If you're experiencing attitude problems with your dog (the pushy dog will often bring his toys to you and demand a game) begin by removing all his toys from the environment. Soon you're going to have children's toys lying around all over the place and having dog toys haphazardly mixed in with them can lead to all sorts of problems (which I'll address in a subsequent section).

Now that your dog no longer has indiscriminate access to his toys you are in a position to control that resource and initiate games with him *if you so choose.* In this context please be aware that chase games of any kind should be avoided altogether. Such games teach your dog that he is faster and stronger than you or your child and this is information he can definitely live without.

Fun and Games

Fun and games are serious business to your dog. Be his portal to pleasure by making him go through you to get them.

As I've just suggested, when it comes to games it's important that *you initiate, control, and end them* at your discretion. Let's see what this means in practical terms. If you like playing fetch with your dog, bring out a toy when you're ready to play, *not when he demands it,* and show it to him. Before you throw it, ask for an obedience command. It can be anything, but make sure you don't throw the toy unless your dog has performed the command nicely. When he brings the toy back and gives it to you (if he doesn't give it up use the "off" command), ask him for a different command and demand compliance before you throw it again. Continue to do this throughout your play session and when you've had enough, end the game by simply putting the toy away. If your dog continues to pester you for more, start running him through short obedience drills. A mind-numbing routine of sit-down-sit-down-stay-sit-stay-down and so on should do the trick. He'll soon get the idea and leave you alone. Whatever games you play with your dog, be sure they all follow this pattern: you initiate, control, and end them.

In relation to this, if your dog has an attitude problem, that is, if he's pushy and demanding, rough-housing, wrestling or other physically competitive games should be temporarily eliminated. As you progress in this program and when you sense that your dog has a more respectful attitude towards you they may be reintroduced so long as the above rules, as well as those that follow, are followed. For example, if you're roughhousing with your dog you should *a)* give him a verbal cue that a game is about to begin such as "okay, let's play,"— without this cue roughhousing should not be allowed since you don't want your dog eventually initiating roughhousing sessions with your child—and *b)* take a break every thirty to forty five seconds, demand a number of obedience commands and then resume the game. During the course of your roughhousing you should also be sure to repeatedly put the dog in a submissive position, that is, on his side or back, with you hovering over him. During this time you should handle him in slightly annoying ways in order to teach him to accept childlike and even inappropriate handling. The idea, of course, is to teach him to accept such handling in stride. *However, you should never allow your child to handle your dog like this.* I will talk about teaching your child to be appropriate with the dog later. The point of these exercises is to build a buffer zone of tolerance into your dog just in case the

Total Control

Initiate, control and end all games at your discretion and they will serve to reinforce your position as leader rather than detract from it. Doing so will also teach your dog to be responsive no matter the level of stimulation.

unexpected happens. Any rebellious behavior on your dog's part should be immediately met with a firm verbal reprimand, a string of obedience commands and a prompt cessation of the fun. During the course of all this you should also *be sure that your dog never uses his teeth* on you in any way. If he does, immediately grab his muzzle and squeeze it shut, issue a loud verbal reprimand, and temporarily cease the game. Spraying him with a squirt bottle can also deter this behavior. You should have a *zero tolerance biting policy*, even during rough play and with a child on the way the reasons should be obvious. In short, by the time your child arrives your dog should have learned never to put his mouth on human skin for any reason, period.

In relation to all this, one will often read that tug-of-war games with dogs should be avoided altogether as they encourage dominance and thus potentially aggressive behavior. My view is that this is a half-truth. If you cannot control the game, definitely don't play it. However, if you can control the game, it can be very useful in asserting your authority over your dog. Let's look at how you can play tug-of-war and have it support your rank management program. As I said, you always initiate the game. Grab the toy and approach the dog, teasing him with it. Give him whatever verbal cue you've decided on to let him know you're now ready to play. As he begins to show interest, demand an obedience command. The moment he executes his command, offer him the toy and begin playing tug-of-war. It's okay to play as hard and rough as you want *provided your dog's teeth are not touching you in any way*—no reckless or careless biting please. Make it difficult for your dog not to bite you by moving the toy quickly and unpredictably and immediately issue a sharp verbal reprimand if he does. Then, run him through a string of obedience commands and quit the game for the time being. The point, of course, is to teach the dog to be *very careful*, even when he's totally worked up. As long as your dog is not recklessly biting, continue to play with him as hard as you want and then suddenly command "off." This should not

Zero-Tolerance

A zero-tolerance biting policy, even in the midst of the roughest play, is an absolute must in your dog's relationship with your child. Be persistent and diligent in enforcing this policy and your dog will be able to take it without dishing it out.

be a problem if you've practiced the exercises I described above. If the dog does not immediately release the toy, spray him in the mouth with Bitter Apple™ spray. This will almost always make him give up the toy instantly. Once he gives it up, promptly issue a command like "sit" or "down." The moment he executes this command you once again offer him the toy and resume playing. Continue like this as long as you like, being sure to demand an "off" and a short string of obedience commands every thirty to forty-five seconds. Played in this way, the tug-of-war game actually supports your rank management program by teaching the dog that you control the entire event. He learns that recklessness is unacceptable, and that by virtue of your authority, an "off" command is all you need in order to gain possession of the precious tug toy. The beauty of this game is that it not only reinforces your dominance, it also teaches your dog to take direction from you when he's extremely excited and helps to channel his intense play and prey drives into obedience commands. This combination of training elements powerfully reinforces your leadership position in the mind of your dog.

Step 10

Do Not Let Your Dog Take Positions Above You

In many ways, dogs are relatively simple and straightforward creatures. This is particularly true in relation to physical postures. Generally speaking, a dog will interpret anyone above him physically as being above him in relation to rank as well. Conversely, anything that is physically below him, he'll tend to view as beneath himself in terms of rank as well. You can use this simple perception to your advantage when addressing issues of social status with your dog. In short, try not to let your dog take up positions above you.

There are many ways in which a dog can assume a position above you. He can jump on top of you when you're lying down. He can climb in your lap and make himself at home

there without an invitation. He can run up a staircase ahead of you and stand at the top looking down at you as you follow him. If you have an interior staircase in your house he might find the stair just above everyone's head and make that a favorite resting place – a convenient vantage point from which he can survey his kingdom.

Taking up positions above you is a meaningful and significant activity for your dog, one that should be curbed when trying to shift his perception of his place in your pack. Doing so is another non-confrontational way to assert your authority over your dog in a way that appeals to his canine sensibilities. For instance, if you're walking up a set of stairs, make the dog hold a sit-stay at the staircase bottom and call him once you're at the top. If you're walking down the stairs, have the dog walk down alongside you (please don't let him bolt down the stairs ahead of you). If your dog is seeking positions in your house such as landings on interior staircases that allow him a vantage point above your head and shoulders, he should be denied access to these areas. If he likes to climb on top of you and lie in your lap uninvited this is a variation on the same theme. While endearing, it is a dominant, pushy and demanding behavior that should be eliminated, or at the very least put under your control. Thus, each time your dog attempts to climb up on you issue a firm "off" command and shove him off or back it up with a squirt bottle if you have to.

A Proper Perspective

Make your dog answer to a "higher power" by taking up positions above him. Looking down on him in this manner means he will have to look up at you and such a posture will do his outlook on your relationship a world of good.

As with furniture rights (see page 20) once your dog no longer takes these things upon himself, you may invite him into your lap if you so desire. The key here is that the choice is yours, not his.

While these things might seem a little harsh, please keep in mind that it will be easy for your dog to get in the habit of rushing up and down stairways recklessly or climbing and laying on top your child, an equally undesirable behavior, potentially endangering him,

GROOM AND HANDLE YOUR DOG REGULARLY

You should be able to handle your dog in any way you see fit. Some dogs can become very sensitive to having certain areas of their bodies handled and may even become aggressive if you insist on touching them there (if your dog has bitten or threatened to bite you in this context please read the section entitled *Dealing with the Serious Problem Dog* on page 92). Additionally, a dog has what are known as *socially sensitive* areas. Primary among these are the upper back and shoulder areas as well as the back of the neck. Others are underneath his chin and along his rear end and hindquarters. Additionally, many dogs have an extreme dislike of having their paws handled. Grooming and handling your dog regularly will not only condition him to accepting various types of handling, it will help you assert your physical domination over him in a potentially pleasurable way. If he is sensitive in relation to such handling you must go through routines of systematic desensitization in order to teach him to take it all in stride. These will be discussed in detail a little further on.

Courtesy: Belinda Levinsen

Additionally, you should be able to place your dog in various submissive positions gently yet firmly, and have him accept such handling. If your dog is small, he should allow you to cradle him like a little baby in your arms—upside-down with your hand on his belly. If he struggles against you, you should firmly restrain him. Once he relaxes, you may gently stroke and pet him teaching him that the end of resistance brings on pleasure and the reduction of stress. If you have a large dog you can place him upside down lengthwise between your legs and achieve the same effect. Similarly, your dog should allow you to place him on his side on the ground and stand over him with your hands gently pinning him to the ground until you release him. While you have him in this position you should be able to give him a thorough body exam and massage. Any mouthing or biting should be met with a firm reprimand and a squirt of the water or Bitter Apple™ spray. These actions, from the perspective of your dog, are physically dominant and therefore significant in relation to rank. As we saw above, if you are able to assert yourself by being physically above your dog while placing him in submissive positions, he will interpret you as socially dominant over him.

Trust and Respect

Trust and respect are the cornerstones of any healthy relationship. Handling your dog regularly will teach him to trust that nothing unpleasant will befall him and respect your right to subject him to such handling. Additionally, it will also help prepare him for handling by your child.

An important note in this context is that you should not attempt these handling exercises with a dog that believes he is firmly entrenched in a leadership position. Doing so could lead to a bite! Before attempting any such exercises with a very dominant dog like this you should be sure that you have diligently implemented every other aspect of this program for some time and have seen a significant change in demeanor on his part. If you are still concerned that your dog might bite or threaten to bite you in this context please read the section entitled *Dealing with the Serious Problem Dog* on page 92.

TEACH AND PRACTICE OBEDIENCE EXERCISES

A great deal of what I've outlined above presumes that your dog understands obedience commands. Clearly, if he doesn't you should begin teaching them immediately. Every dog's vocabulary, in my view, should, at a minimum, include the commands sit, down, stay, come, and off. Additionally, your dog should walk nicely on the leash and be generally attentive towards you. More advanced commands would include stand-stay, heel, and down out of motion and at a distance. I assure you that every dog can learn these commands regardless of age, breed, or previous history. The only exception would clearly be a geriatric dog who is essentially senile and physically incapacitated.

Down-stay!

While this isn't the place to go into an extensive discussion of teaching obedience commands I'll share one exercise of self-control that I view as indispensable and which is surprisingly easy to teach. It's the *sixty-minute* down-stay. Now, you might be thinking, "sixty minutes—no way! Not possible!" But it's easier than you think. Select an hour period of time during the evening—perhaps while watching your favorite television program—put your dog on a leash and into a down-stay near you. Put one foot on the leash so that your dog can't get far if he decides to move, have the handle in your hand, and then relax and watch your program. Your dog may lie down and sleep if he likes, he can watch TV if he's that sort, but he is not to get up *under any circumstances*. If he tries to get up, which he inevitably will in the beginning, quickly place him back in his down-stay and start over. Most dogs get it rather quickly but *no matter how long it takes, stay with it*. Once he does it in one situation try it in another one. And then another. Imagine how helpful this will be when you're trying to get something done with your new child, like nursing.

Obedience exercises are crucial to the development of a proper relationship with any dog, but they are utterly indispensable if you're planning to have your dog live with a new child in the household. If your dog has no understanding of obedience commands he will most likely end up spending a great deal of time isolated from the new social situation and, as stated above, this is something you want to avoid at all costs. Isolation will only teach the dog that his life took a radical turn for the worse the day your baby arrived. If your dog's understanding of obedience commands is limited, now might be a good time to hire a trainer or attend some classes.

A SPRINGBOARD TO THE FUTURE

As I mentioned before, this rank management program will build a foundation from which you can resolve most potential behavior problems in your dog long before the arrival of your child. And even if you're not experiencing any real problems with your dog the rules set forth above are almost indispensable if you're going to have a small child around. After all, do you want your dog jumping up on everyone, stealing food, refusing to obey commands, climbing all over the furniture or demanding games from you or your child? Of course not. A dog like this will inevitably be relegated to the fringe of your life rather than being integrated as part of the family unit.

If you are experiencing behavior problems such as the ones alluded to at the beginning of this chapter, or any others, you may find that simply implementing the program outlined above may diminish or even entirely eliminate them. This is due to the fact that once the dog understands that his position is at the bottom of your pack he will no longer feel compelled to act as if he were at the top. If this type of compulsion was driving his problem behaviors they may just dissolve. If they don't, at least you've laid the foundation for dissolving them. In the next section we'll look at a number of exercises that will help to eliminate a variety of problem behaviors that would make having the dog in the presence of a child a bad idea.

A Hailing Frequency

"Open a channel!" are Captain Picard's famous words when contacting an alien species. Obedience training opens a channel of communication between you and your dog, one that facilitates inter-species relationships and understanding. "Make it so!"

Summary of the Doggie Twelve-Step Program

1. Make him work for a living and play hard to get.

2. Control feeding arrangements so you eat before the dog *and he knows it*!

3. Control sleeping and resting areas.

4. Make the dog move out of your way at least ten to fifteen times a day.

5. Control access to narrow openings. Make your dog look to you for direction when embarking on any new ventures.

6. Do not let your dog pull ahead of you on the leash. Be a leader and lead!

7. Do not let the dog jump all over you or anyone else as a form of greeting.

8. Do not let the dog take food from you or any place in the home without your permission. Teach a solid "off" command.

9. Control the games the dog is allowed to play. Remember, you initiate, control and end all games.

10. Do not let the dog take positions above you.

11. Groom and handle your dog regularly.

12. Teach and practice obedience exercises. Include long down-stays in his daily routine.

A Final Thought

Please understand that dogs crave structure, guidance, and authority. Therefore, the person who puts the most pressure and demands on a dog *in a fair way* will get the lion's share of the dog's love, affection, and respect. That should be you! This chapter has shown you how to put yourself in that position if you weren't already there. By being your dog's leader you are well-positioned to guide him into his new life with your child.

ADDRESSING AND RESOLVING POTENTIAL BEHAVIOR PROBLEMS

 If you reread the list of questions raised at the beginning of the previous chapter, you'll find that many problematic issues were addressed through the implementation of the rank management program. For example, if your dog's disposition was pushy and demanding, if he was jumping up on you, begging incessantly at the table, climbing all over the furniture, or pulling you down the street like a sled dog, this should all have changed once you started applying the principles of rank management since they directly address these issues. If these behaviors haven't been resolved then you haven't yet implemented the program properly and you might want to revisit that section.

In this chapter we'll take a look at what's left over. Specifically, I'll address the following questions:
- What if my dog doesn't like children? (page 52)
- What if my dog is afraid of sudden movements, loud noises, or any disruption of his immediate environment? (page 58)
- What if my dog is snappy and reactive to being touched in certain ways? (page 60)
- What if he's afraid of being left alone and generally emotionally dependent? (page 64)
- What if he's possessive over toys or food? (page 73)
- What if my dog barks excessively? (page 81)
- What if he's overly protective? (page 87)
- What if I have several dogs and they don't get along so well together? (page 89)

Let's take a few moments to investigate these questions and come up with some solutions. However, please keep in mind that in order for the solutions outlined below to truly work you should have already implemented the rank management program described above. If you haven't, it's likely that what is discussed below will produce, at best, marginal results. After all, you can't build a building without a first floor and rank management is the first floor of a comprehensive and thorough approach to behavior modification.

Additionally, *the solutions provided below for issues that potentially involve aggression are primarily designed for dogs in whom these problems could be described as mild to moderate.* If you would describe your dog's problem as somewhere between moderate and severe please read the section entitled *Dealing with the Serious Problem Dog* on page 92. Bearing all this in mind, let's get started.

What if my dog doesn't like children?

There are many reasons dogs don't like kids, but most of them revolve around lack of early socialization with them. Additionally, children's noisiness and generally unpredictable nature can make many dogs apprehensive and often some unpleasant experience with a child in the dog's history may have contributed to his general aversion. (If your dog has bitten or threatened to bite children please read the section entitled *Dealing with the Serious Dog Problem* on page 92) Whatever the case, the solution is the same: you must gradually get the dog used to the presence of children in increments he can tolerate. The goal, of course, is to teach him first that children are not a threat but rather a potential source of pleasurable experiences, and second, that there are acceptable ways of interacting with them.

There are two types of canine temperaments to consider: the fearful one and the dominant, pushy and overly exuberant one. Let's start with the more common, the fearful one. Whenever dealing with issues of fear in a dog you must prove to him systematically that "the only thing to fear is fear itself." Since your dog doesn't speak English you can't simply say to him, "Hey, don't sweat it, no one is going to hurt you here."

GRRRR!

Instead you must prove to him through repeated experience that there's nothing to worry about. What this means practically is that you must expose him to levels of the offending stimulus (i.e., children), that he can tolerate and help him connect that experience to something positive. This approach is known as "systematic desensitization" and is key to dealing with all sorts of fear-based behavior issues. Be aware that approaches using systematic desensitization can often take a lot of time. Don't be impatient here. Slow, incremental progress is what you're looking for, not overnight results. Sometimes systematic desensitization can take months to produce solid results and trying to rush it will only set you back. All the more reason to get started sooner rather than later.

Now, let's take a look at how you can make something like this work. The first thing you're going to need to do is find some kids. This is often easier said than done since not too many moms are going to be willing to let you use their child as a training distraction for your dog. What I usually suggest to my clients is to find an area where children are commonly present, such as a school or playground.

Once you find such an area you want to position yourself with your dog at some distance from the kids. At this distance, the dog should be aware of the children but not exhibit any signs of fear. Once there simply ask your dog to sit and begin feeding him treats. (If your dog is not so excited about food, skipping a meal or two and bringing out killer treats like hot dogs or cheese will usually solve the problem). It's important that the dog only get treats while he's aware of the children in the environment because you're trying to get him to associate the presence of children with good things from you. This serves several purposes. First, and most obvious, it teaches him to expect something good in the presence of children thus helping to dissolve his fear and second, it puts his attention on you and removes it from the children. In other

Face the Fear and Do It Anyway

Fear is the root cause of an overwhelming percentage of aggression in dogs. In order to teach your dog that "the only thing to fear is fear itself" you must patiently implement routines of "systematic desensitization" over a sustained period of time. Thus, as with most things, there's no time like the present to get started.

words, it takes his focus away from something he's worried about, and puts it on something which he views as a comforting and reassuring presence, you! Once the dog is relatively at ease with this arrangement and not showing any signs of fear, it's time to move a little closer. Be sure to move closer only in increments the dog can tolerate. You want to *avoid crossing his fear threshold at all costs* as this will only set you back. When you've found the right position, repeat the above procedure. Once you've got your dog's attention focused on you and the treats begin asking him for obedience commands. The more he's focused on you and has something to do the less he'll be worried about the kids. If at any point you see that your dog is beginning to become anxious about the children, go ahead and put some distance between you and them. Again, you want to be sure not to cross your dog's fear threshold and avoid making him feel trapped by forcing too much on him too fast.

Keep repeating this procedure, always in amounts and increments that your dog can tolerate, and eventually you'll find yourselves very near the children. How long this will take depends on two things: the level of fear in your dog and the frequency of your outings with him. The more you go out with him, the faster he will begin to get over it (nonetheless, it could take weeks to months, so please be patient). As you find yourselves getting closer and closer to the children inevitably a child will want to come up and say hello to your dog. What you do at this time will be a judgment call. As already stated, if your dog has a propensity to bite in situations in which he's not entirely comfortable read the section below entitled *Dealing with the Serious Problem Dog* on page 92 before going any further. Another factor to consider is the child. Is he or she old enough to follow your directions in relating to your dog? If not, then you might just say that your dog is scared of children and pass on the interaction. On the other hand, if your dog is not inclined to bite and has been making good progress with these exercises you may give the child several treats and ask him or her to offer them to your dog. *Tell the child not to attempt to pet your dog but to allow the dog to reach for the treat.* If you see that your dog is experiencing significant resistance to the whole idea then abort the exercise. If not, then allow him to take treats from the child. If you're nervous about this aspect of the exercise try finding a fenced in playground where you can locate yourself on one side of the fence with your dog and have kids give him treats from the other side. This way, everyone is safe and often progress can be made a lot faster and with a lot less tension.

Once your dog has reached the stage where he will accept treats from one or more children through the fence in a very relaxed manner, you're making great progress in dealing with his fear. Nonetheless, take your time before you have children give him treats without the benefit of the fence. However, once your dog is readily taking treats from children and you've gotten to the point where the fence is no longer necessary, you want to be sure to give proper instructions to the children with regards to interacting with and touching your dog. First, ask them not to approach the dog, but to let the dog approach them. Additionally, instruct them not to bend over your dog and not to pet him on top of his head. Rather, have them stand with their side to the dog, reach out their hand and, *if your dog is okay with it*, pet him under his chin and neck. This will appear much less dominant and threatening and will do a lot to put your dog at ease. Also, ask them to move slowly and deliberately rather than with sudden and sharp motions. Once you've arrived at this point you're in pretty good shape, but don't rest here. Keep doing these exercises until your dog shows absolutely no fear of the presence of children. If you've been working in the same context up until now, (i.e., the same school or playground,) try going to a new situation and see if what your dog has learned transfers to that situation. If not, you may have to

Little by Little

I often tell my clients that in dog training progress is always made on the increment. What this means is that progress is usually not made in great leaps and bounds but in tiny little steps. Nowhere is this more true than in approaches using systematic desensitization. Ironically, working slowly for results will produce them faster than trying to rush it which will almost always set you back. Remember the tortoise and the hare: slow but steady wins the race!

backtrack a little in the new situation until the dog gets comfortable in that one. When that's done find another and so on. I cannot overemphasize the importance of frequency in relation to these exercises. You simply cannot do them too often. Even after you have your child, you should continue to try to do them since at some point your child is going to be bringing home little friends. "Too much is never enough," should be your guiding philosophy here, so keep working.

If your dog's issue isn't fear, but instead pushy and dominant or overly exuberant behavior, you must follow a different approach. First, consider whether your dog is getting sufficient exercise. Lack of exercise is a leading contributor to problem behaviors. There is a great deal of truth to the old adage that tired dogs are good dogs. There's simply less energy to throw around. In addition, obedience training is indispensable and you should have implemented the rank management program described above. If your dog doesn't respect you and doesn't understand obedience commands, you'll have practically no chance of teaching him to approach children appropriately without relating to them in a dominant or pushy fashion. On the other hand, once these elements are in place you should have an easy time of it. In the same way described above, you should begin by bringing your dog into situations where children are present. Starting at a distance where the children don't provide too much of a distraction begin working your dog with his obedience commands (which he should already know). The most important commands to focus on are sit, down and stay. Be sure your dog is aware of the children, but that they don't provide too much of a distraction. Also, be sure that your approach to training is fun and positive for your dog. You don't want him to associate the presence of children with harsh obedience exercises. Once your dog performs his commands reliably – that is, on the first command and without corrections – in whatever proximity you started with, try working him a little closer. Once he's okay with that, move closer yet again. Eventually you should be able to work your dog very close to children. If the children begin showing an interest in your dog, hand them a few treats and have them ask him for his obedience commands. If your dog suddenly won't obey, demand the behavior from him yourself and of course, if he starts jumping or lunging you should give him a collar correction and place him immediately back in a sit-stay or a down-stay. Doing this consistently will teach your dog to associate the presence of children with a particular type of behavior: obedient. This is called "situational learning." In other words, your dog will begin to associate a particular situation (i.e., being around children) with obedience exercises, sometimes demanded by you and sometimes by the kids. If he also learns that performing obedience commands for kids will often produce treats, he will soon develop a very positive outlook on the entire situation. In short, when your dog sees kids, he's going to think that sit, down and stay will mean treats and affection and will soon start offering these behaviors on his own. What could be better than that?

Courtesy: Belinda Levinsen

In both of the above situations, you are teaching your dog a new set of expectations and responses when he becomes aware of the presence of children. Once these expectations are internalized, the likelihood of having trouble with him around kids will be radically diminished. Once again, in the beginning the more you practice the better, and while you'll need to do less of this as your dog gets accustomed to it, it's always good to make this part of his daily or weekly routine. This is your best insurance policy against any future problems.

WHAT IF MY DOG IS AFRAID OF, OR AGGRESSIVE TOWARDS, SUDDEN MOVEMENTS, LOUD NOISES, OR ANY DISRUPTION OF HIS IMMEDIATE ENVIRONMENT?

Aaargh! Make it go away! Pleeze!

The answer to this question is essentially the same as to the one above: your dog needs to undergo a process of systematic desensitization. He must get used to these stimuli in slow increments that he can handle. Again, the dog's responses can be divided into essentially two types: fearful, and pushy or dominant. If your dog has bitten or threatened to bite in this context please read the section entitled *Dealing with the Serious Problem Dog* on page 92.

With a shy dog, the approach is identical to what I've just outlined: bring the dog into the presence of the offending stimulus, be it a certain type of noise, movement, or any other disruption, in doses he can handle without generating a fearful response and then begin giving him treats. Teach him to associate the presence of the stimulus with something wonderful from you and add small increments of the stimulus as the dog's ability to handle it increases. As with the above, take your time and always allow the dog room to back out of a situation if he feels threatened. Having him focused on you through obedience commands will decrease the likelihood of a fearful response simply because a good part of his attention will be on you and therefore not on the fear-provoking stimulus.

If your dog's response to novel stimulation is to lunge, bark, or react in a pushy and dominant way, you should also expose him to the stimulation in increments that do no make him reactive and try to associate it with treats. However, you will most likely also have to sharply reprimand him for any outburst. In fact, I tend to feel that if the dog has not been effectively corrected for his outbursts he may never learn that you really don't like them, even if you're teaching him to build a new set of associations. In other words, I feel it's important to at least a few times put the dog in a situation that will guarantee an outburst and then effectively correct him for it. The best way I know of to reprimand a dog without real physical force is with a squirt bottle filled with Bitter Apple™ spray, a taste deterrent readily available at most pet shops. The breath spray Binaca™ will also work quite well with most dogs. But there's no reason that a collar correction couldn't appropriately and efficiently achieve the same thing. By communicating your disapproval of the behavior to the dog you will cause him to inhibit his response and thus put an initial break in it. Once that's done you can teach him a new set of responses. As an example, let's say your dog is reactive—he jumps or barks—if a guest suddenly gets up from the sofa. The moment he makes a reactive move you should squirt him in the nose and mouth with Bitter Apple™ spray or give him a sharp snap on the collar and strongly tell him "no." If you do find yourself forced to give the dog a snap on the collar, please be sure to find the level of force that's just enough to deter the dog and communicate your displeasure to him *with one or two corrections.* Anything more is abusive as is anything less, since you'll only have to dish out additional corrections.

Set this situation up as often as feasible and continue to reprimand your dog until he begins to inhibit himself. Now, many people believe that once the dog is no longer producing the behavior the problem is resolved. However, in my view the problem isn't truly resolved until you can successfully undermine the core motivation that caused the dog to act out in the first place. Once again, the only way to do that is by teaching him a new set of associations through positive feedback, in other words, connecting something wonderful (such as a treat) to the offending stimulus. Continuing with the above example, now that your dog is no longer reactive to your guest suddenly getting up because he's worried about your reprimand, begin giving him a treat every time the person gets up. Soon, he'll forget about why he was upset in the first place and simply be looking around for his treat. This same approach applies to any item to which your dog is reactive such as skateboards, bicycles, garbage trucks, etc. Only when he's both inhibiting himself and solidly conditioned to expect something positive in relation to the offending event should you consider the behavior resolved. As he gets more and more conditioned to the new set of expectations, you can begin fading out the treats since the dog will have learned that the sudden movements or loud noises present no threat to him and that any kind of outbursts won't be tolerated. As with the last issue, you want to practice these routines as often as possible and continue to do so even after there is no longer an apparent problem. Again, "too much is never enough" is a good motto here.

WHAT IF MY DOG IS SENSITIVE AND REACTIVE TO BEING TOUCHED IN CERTAIN WAYS?

Again, systematic desensitization is the order of the day. You want to teach your dog to associate the handling with something positive and through the course of repeated experiences learn to trust that kind of handling. If your dog has

A Total Solution

Teaching a dog to inhibit undesirable behaviors through force or compulsion alone is usually an incomplete way of resolving the problem. You should seek to undermine the core motivations driving the behavior through heavy doses of positive reinforcement in order to arrive at a complete and reliable solution.

bitten or threatened to bite you in this context please read the section entitled *Dealing with the Serious Problem Dog* on page 92. If your dog has not gone this far but you think he may at some point, please read on.

With a dog that is sensitive to having certain body parts touched you should initiate an interaction by simply giving him a few treats. The best treats are those that he can continue to nibble and chew on while you're pursuing the exercise. For example, hot dogs or string cheese are excellent choices. Simply hold the entire thing in your hand and continue to feed it out to him as he nibbles away at it. Once he's focused on the treat and while he's busy working at it *slowly* move your other hand towards whatever area is sensitive. If at any point you sense that your dog is becoming wary, back off and simply hold your hand in an area where he is aware of it but not in any way reactive or even suspicious. Soon he will begin to ignore that hand and continue to take treats. As he does this again move your hand ever so slowly and gently closer to his sensitive area until you are actually touching it. Once you've touched him and held the touch for a few moments remove both your hand and the treats from your dog simultaneously. At this point, he will usually stare at the hand that had the treats in it eagerly awaiting more. After letting his anticipation build for a few moments, again present the hand with the treat in it. Once he's focused here, again slowly bring your other hand to the sensitive area. Continue touching him there for a few moments and then remove both hands again. Repeat this procedure until your dog becomes more and more comfortable with the whole routine. Most dogs will learn relatively quickly to ignore the hand that's touching them. At this point, start adding speed to the exercise. In other words, begin moving your non-treat hand in more and more quickly, really reaching for your dog's sensitive area, as he continues to be focused on the treat and his trust in the exercise builds. Continue adding speed until

Courtesy: Kimberly Burke

you can move your hand towards your dog's sensitive area with the same speed as someone who might suddenly reach out and pet him. Throughout this time continue to present the treat to the dog at least a few seconds *before* your hand actually touches him so more of his focus is on the treat rather than being touched.

Once this routine is solidly established, start changing the pattern by making the increment of time between getting the dog focused on the treat and touching him shorter and shorter. In other words, if the dog was focused on the treat for ten seconds before touching him you should now cut that back to nine. Then cut back to eight and seven and so on until there is only a one second interval between the time the dog starts getting his treats and is being reached for (very quickly). Ultimately the time will come when you can present the treat to your dog at the very same moment that you're reaching for him. Because he will, at this point, have had somewhere between dozens and hundreds of exposures to this exercise he will be very relaxed about it and will have learned to ignore the hand that is reaching for him. Before moving to the next step, you want to be sure that you're really solid on this one. Spend some time repeating this step over and over until the dog is perfectly habituated to it.

The next step involves *reaching for him first* and then presenting the treat. At first, the time increment between reaching for him and giving him the treat should be minuscule, a quarter of a second perhaps. Then, start working your way up to a second, then two, three and so on. Pursued systematically, you'll soon be able to wait five or even ten seconds *after touching your dog* to give him his treat until eventually you won't need a treat at all. At this point, he will have so strongly learned to associate having someone touch his sensitive area that when he sees the hand coming he will already be looking for his treat. Since in the thousands of times that he will have been reached for during the course of these exercises he will never have had a bad experience with it, he'll develop an enormous degree of trust in the entire process. Moreover, he will now view the entire experience in a very positive light. Once your dog is totally comfortable with you and your family doing this start having friends do it with him as often as possible as well. And if you can get any kids to help out that would be even better. In each case you may have to start at square one but once your dog has learned to trust the entire process with one person it will be a lot easier for him to trust the next one, and then the next one, and so on. The idea is that when the day comes that someone reaches for your dog outside the context of this exercise, he'll just assume that it's the same old game again and be totally relaxed about it.

Courtesy: Jane Reed

Once you've managed to condition your dog to being touched in sensitive areas it would be a good idea to take all this one step further and begin to roughhouse with him as described on page 42. If you'll recall, there I talked about interacting with the dog in slightly annoying ways in order to teach him to accept childlike handling. If you can get your touch sensitive dog to take this all in stride you've come a long way indeed.

As with the other exercises in desensitization, how long this all takes depends on your dog. When fear issues are involved you must be patient and work at your dog's pace rather than at the pace you'd like to see it work. The fact is that the slower and more systematically you work, paradoxically, the faster you get results.

WHAT IF MY DOG IS EMOTIONALLY DEPENDENT AND AFRAID OF BEING LEFT ALONE?

Pleeze don't leave me.

The dog that is emotionally dependent on his owner (always underfoot – can't make a move without you) or has problems with *separation anxiety* is also the dog that is potentially going to have the greatest difficulty adjusting to the arrival of a child. A dog suffering from separation anxiety has difficulty tolerating being left alone, which often results in nuisance barking, destructive behavior, or elimination in the house. The same dog often also has difficulty with the idea that he is not the center of your universe. Clearly, once your child arrives your dog will necessarily no longer be the focal point of your affections to the degree that he is now. In this context, it's very easy for him to interpret your child's arrival as the source of his perceived deterioration in his relationship with you. In order to avoid this, it's important to deal with emotional neediness and separation anxiety as long before the arrival of the child as possible so that the inevitable changes in your relationship are not associated with the birth of your baby. And, changes in the nature of your relationship are precisely what's called for. Specifically, the emotional nature of the relationship with your dog needs to be toned down and he needs to be conditioned to accept increasing periods of time away from you. I understand that this may be difficult for many people, but keep in mind that the attention you now shower on him will soon be flowing towards your new child, potentially leaving the dog feeling left out in the cold.

Even if your dog isn't really overly emotionally dependent or suffering from separation anxiety, the implementation of the program outlined below, perhaps in a diluted form, would be advisable anyway since normally the arrival of a baby puts serious limitations on the amount of time you can spend with your dog. Again, you want to do everything possible to avoid having your dog associate these changes with the arrival of your child.

So the obvious question is: how do you tone down the sometimes overly emotional and dependent nature of the relationship with such a dog and teach him to spend increasing periods of time alone? The answer, as with most things in behavior modification, is in small increments. If your dog has the tendency to follow you around like a shadow begin by having him hold down-stays for just a few moments as you go from one place to another. If he does not know "down-stay" you can simply tie him to something like the leg of a sofa or table and ask him to "wait". The important thing is to leave only for *a brief period of time*. How long that is varies from dog to dog, but it should be a period he can tolerate with as little stress as possible. For some dogs that might mean two seconds. Whatever it is, that's what you work with. When you return to the dog's proximity you should simply ignore him, that is, *don't look at him, don't speak to him, and don't touch him.* Just be in his space while keeping the level of interaction to a minimum. This is what I mean when I say toning down the emotional nature of your relationship. If you're constantly coddling, petting and talking to the dog he's addicted to that constant level of attention—precisely what you're trying to wean him away from.

Once you've returned to the dog's proximity, you shouldn't wait too long to depart yet again. If your first departure consisted of all of two seconds, then maybe it's three seconds this time. It all depends on your dog. Again, you want to *be sure to return before he crosses his fear threshold.* Repeat this procedure as often as possible, slowly working to increase the increments of time for which he can be left alone. You'll find that the time it takes you to get from two seconds to five minutes will be much longer than the time it takes to get from five minutes to ten minutes and so on. As the dog learns to ignore your comings and goings—because they are now so frequent—it will become easier and easier for him to tolerate increasing amounts of time alone.

Is this Natural?

Of all the unnatural things we ask our dogs to do such as heel, sit, down, stay, etc. perhaps there is none more difficult than asking them to spend long periods of time alone. Dogs, like humans, are pack animals and in a natural setting will spend every moment of their lives surrounded by their pack members. However, to live successfully in a human world your dog must learn to spend time alone. Do him a favor and make alone time a daily part of his routine. Doing so will put him at ease and prevent innumerable difficult behavior problems.

If you want to make the entire affair a bit more appealing to him try tossing him a treat just before you get up and leave, but be very low key about it. Simply drop it there on your way out of the area. Remember, no speaking to, touching, or looking at your dog. Just leave. Dropping a treat on your way out will help focus your dog on something positive rather than on the fact that you're leaving and help him to begin to build a positive association with your departure. As you increase the periods of time that you leave your dog, you can replace the treat with a favorite, food related, toy *that he only gets* when you leave the area. As soon as you return, you pick up the toy *and continue to ignore the dog.* This will teach him that he only has access to this special thing when you're gone and avoid getting him emotionally charged up upon your return. Your arrival means the toy goes away. Some suggestions for toys include Kong Toys™ stuffed with cheese, meat, peanut butter or anything else that your dog loves, a hollow marrow bone filled with the same, Planet Toys™, Buster Cubes™ and other things along those lines. A cut up pig's ear stuffed into a Kong Toy™ is my latest favorite. Whatever it is, it should be something that the dog really likes and *that he gets at no other time.* Using this approach your dog will learn, over time, that when you leave you'll soon be back and that he has a window of opportunity here to get something wonderful. Repeating this exercise as often as possible will help your dog develop the emotional stamina and trust to be left alone for increasingly long periods.

Once you've reached some baseline success with your dog, begin leaving him in different parts of the house for longer and longer periods so that he doesn't associate alone time with just one place. Also, during the times that you're not explicitly doing these exercises be sure to wean the dog off your affections. If he's always in your lap, on the sofa next to you, or in your bed at night, begin restricting such interactions now with the goal of eliminating them almost altogether. This might sound extreme. After all, if you can't cuddle

Courtesy: Belinda Levinson

with your dog and be affectionate with him what's the point of having him? But the point is really to teach him not to need these things in order to feel emotionally secure. Once you've gotten him to the point where he can feel emotionally secure without these props, you can reintroduce all these interactions in measured doses and in a way that they don't create a dependency. To feel emotionally insecure is a terrible state to be in, so what this program calls for is the temporary sacrificing of your own emotional need to be physically close with your dog for the sake of his mental health and well being.

Now, all that having been said, it's important to keep in mind what I said a moment ago, which is to *cut down your affection in small increments*. The idea is to wean him off your affections, not simply to cut him off. For example, if your dog has been sleeping in the bed with you for the last six years, don't start by putting him in the garage or you're guaranteed to have a full blown meltdown on your hands, which will set your efforts back enormously. Instead, start by putting a dog bed next to your own and tying him to the foot of your bed so he's got enough room to get comfy but can't jump back up under the covers with you. Once he's okay with that, begin scooting his bed further and further away from your own until he can sleep just outside your bedroom door. Similarly, if your dog is always on your lap or on the sofa next to you, begin by having him at your feet and off the sofa. Then, perhaps using the same dog bed, you can condition him to staying further and further away. Throughout all of this be sure to wean him off the petting, cooing and general coddling as well.

Having outlined the above, let's take a look at a few potential bumps in the road and how to deal with them. The first one relates to the dog who starts whining, barking and complain-

For the Greater Good!

"To feel emotionally insecure is a terrible state to be in, so what this program calls for is the temporary sacrificing of your own emotional need to be physically close with your dog for the sake of his mental health and well being."

ing the absolute moment he senses he's alone. While, as I said above, the goal is to attempt to return to your dog before he hits his anxiety threshold there are times when, despite your best efforts your dog will resort to a variety of attention-getting behaviors almost immediately. Usually he does this because he's found that in the past they worked. However, now is the time to learn that they'll work no longer, that there is a behavior boundary that you will not allow him to cross. If your dog begins to bark you can: *a)* quickly rush back into the room, squirt him in the mouth and nose area with water or Bitter Apple™ spray, firmly tell him "quiet," and then immediately leave the room; *b)* rush back into the room and put him through a mind numbing obedience drill such as sit-down-sit-stand-down, etc. until he gets visibly bored. Demand tight compliance and when you've pushed the dog beyond the point where he's had enough, leave the room once more. He might decide that it's better to be left with his Kong Toy™ than to be drilled like this by you. With regard to the concern that negative attention is better than no attention, in other words, your dog is still getting a payoff from your presence, even if it's unpleasant – I don't buy it. If you make your responses unpleasant enough at some point your dog will cease and desist. However, there are a couple of other options that you can explore without having to go back to your dog: *c)* slam your hand loudly against a nearby door, wall, or any other item likely to startle the dog; or *d)* loudly rattle a shake can (empty soda can with five or six pennies in it) without saying a word. One of these approaches will work with most dogs.

An additional area of importance to consider in the resolution of separation anxiety is that of departures and homecomings. In these situations, you should be sure to ignore your dog for ten to fifteen minutes before leaving and ten to fifteen minutes after returning home. Departures that involve a lot of interaction with the dog merely serve to work him up emotionally just before you leave. The moment that door

Playing it Cool

Toning down departures and homecomings by ignoring your dog for fifteen minutes before you leave and for at least a few minutes after your return home will help to avoid the emotional spikes that can lead to attacks of separation anxiety.

closes behind you he feels as if he's been left hung out to dry, and his anxiety level can go through the roof. Enthusiastic returns are similar in that they merely serve to highlight for the dog the vast difference between when you're there and when you're not. Of course, the whole idea is to narrow the qualitative difference between when you're there and when you're not so your dog can avoid the wild emotional swings that lead to attacks of anxiety.

To further diffuse the concern your dog may experience around your departures it can be helpful to teach him to ignore what are known as "pre-departure cues." In other words, most dogs are intensely aware of the patterns that lead up to your departure such as getting your coat out of the closet, putting on your shoes, the jingle of keys, etc. These events can often trigger anxiety attacks, so reducing their relevance to your dog, in addition to ignoring him before your departure can be very helpful. As with many of the exercises described in this section, this one is also simple but some-what tedious. The trick is to go through your pre-departure routine as often as possible without actually leaving. For example, pick up and jingle your keys, and then set them down again. Go to the closet and pull out your coat only to hang it up again. Of course, totally ignore the dog throughout all this. As often as possible string all these events together in the exact sequence that you follow when you actually leave and if you can do this at times of the day that you normally leave without leaving, so much the better. The more often you do this, the quicker it will help your dog dissolve his anxiety over your departures.

That'll do humans.

A related issue that often arises with needy dogs is the inability to tolerate anyone besides them getting affection. For instance, it's not uncommon for a dog to become annoyed and intrusive if two members of the household are exchanging displays of affection such as hugs. Many dogs will start barking, trying to push their way between the owners , or pursue any attention-getting behavior that will cause the affectionate displays to cease. I've even had clients whose dogs won't let them talk on the phone without throwing a fit. The problems in relation to raising a child under these circumstances are obvious. You should teach your dog that such interruptions are unacceptable and then teach him to build a new and positive association with affectionate displays between household members. Begin by setting up as many displays of affection as possible (this is the fun part) and reprimanding your dog for any intrusions. My definition of an intrusion is coming within five feet of where the affectionate incident is taking place, and then engaging in barking or anything else annoying. My favorite method of response, once again, is the trusty squirt bottle filled with either water or Bitter Apple™ spray. If your dog gets too close, in a firm tone command "out" and squirt him in the nose and mouth. For most dogs, this sudden shock will give them pause for reflection. A few more repetitions and you'll likely begin to see the behavior subside. If your dog likes to bark for attention, I suggest you begin by tying him near the area where your staged display takes place and squirting him for barking as described in the section dealing with barking dogs (page 81). The leash will prevent your dog from running away in order to avoid your reprimand when you go to spray him. It will also keep him from getting a chase game out of the deal.

Courtesy: Bari Halperin

Once you've managed to suppress your dog's annoying interruptions you can take the next step of teaching him to look forward to displays of affection by helping him build new and positive associations with them. Simply set it up so that just as the staged affections begin taking place, he gets a favorite bone, toy or treat to chew on. When the affectionate displays are over, remove the item from the dog. This will help him to quickly associate the two events and teach him that good things happen to him when others display affection. Moreover, those good things happen at some distance from you. As his views begin to change you'll need to do less and less of this and eventually your dog will be totally comfortable not being the center of the known universe.

In addition to everything discussed above, the extreme importance of exercise should not be ignored. The old saying, "tired dogs are good dogs," is true indeed. If your dog has a lot of pent up energy that he hasn't had the opportunity to release, it's guaranteed that energy is going to be easily translated and channeled into his anxiety. On the other hand, if he is exhausted, he simply will not have as much energy available to fuel his fear. In other words, exhaustion is more readily translated into sleep. Sleeping dogs don't worry about the whereabouts of their owners. They dream dog dreams and are thus otherwise occupied. Therefore, working with your dog in all the routines outlined above is going to be much more effective when done in the context of exhaustion.

Finally, there are some dogs who, despite your best efforts, are so deeply anxious that they are virtually impossible to rehabilitate with conventional methods of behavior modification. It seems that no matter how much work you do with them the results are never better than marginal. In those cases it might be advisable to consider anti-anxiety medication. Such medications can provide a bridge and allow you to gain a foothold in the resolution of the dog's fear. They can create an opening and receptivity on the part of your dog that simply was not there before. With this opening, the effects of your exercises will be radically improved. However, it is important to note that the anti-anxiety medications, at least in the way that I view them, are not a solution in and of themselves. They are an aid to the routines outlined above. If, through the use of such medications, you can get your dog to relax enough to develop the new habits and associations built by these training exercises, then, after the dog has had sufficient exposure to the exercises you should be able to wean him off the medications. The exercises will have created new learned behaviors and associations that will hopefully

Just Say Maybe!
The following medications are all effective at relieving anxiety and new ones are coming out all the time. Speak to your veterinarian about which of them might be appropriate for your dog and never use any medication without the advice of a vet. In other words, please don't share your Prozac™.

- *Elavil™ (amitriptyline)*
- *Clomicalm™ (clomipramine)*
- *Prozac™ (fluoxetine)*

stick once the dog is taken off the medications. How long this takes can be hard to say, but I usually advise my clients to prepare for six months of work when attempting to resolve issues involving extreme emotional dependency and separation anxiety. That is not to say that things can't be resolved sooner, it just prepares one psychologically for the possibility that they might not be and will hopefully give them the resolve to keep trying. With respect to medications, since there are new ones coming out all the time and they are available only through prescription, you should speak with your veterinarian about them. If your vet is not that knowledgeable about these substances ask him or her to recommend someone who is.

All that having been said, let's take a moment to summarize the program in simple terms.

- Begin by toning down the overly emotional nature of the relationship you have with your dog. Do this using the above described exercises, but be sure to implement them in increments your dog can handle. Just cutting your dog off from affection can actually kick him into a full blown anxiety attack and set your efforts back enormously. Remember the tortoise and the hare: slow but steady wins the race.
- Try to build new associations for your dog with what it means to be alone by providing positive experiences in your absence.
- Also, do what you reasonably can to exercise and tire the dog.
- Additionally, if necessary, investigate the use of anti-anxiety medications to help make inroads with your dog's anxiety issues.
- Finally, give yourself as much time as possible to make this work. Don't start with these exercises two weeks before your baby is due, or worse, after your baby's arrival. By then it may be too late. Start now!

WHAT IF MY DOG IS POSSESSIVE OVER TOYS OR FOOD?

Object and food guarding is perhaps one of the most common and most dangerous issues facing dogs and children. Since dogs often view children as lower ranking pack members and also as potential competitors for valued resources, the likelihood of trouble here should be taken especially seriously. If your dog has bitten or threatened to bite you or other dogs in this context please read the section entitled *Dealing with the Serious Problem Dog* on page 92.

Mine!

If your dog gets tense around objects or food but has not bitten or threatened to then read on. For starters, you should be sure that you've implemented the doggie twelve-step program described in the last chapter. After all, if your dog is guarding objects against you the first question you should ask yourself is why he feels he has the right to do this. Clearly he doesn't respect you as leader so that's the place to start. Once that's accomplished proceed as outlined below. You must teach your dog to both trust you and expect something positive when you approach him around food and favorite objects. By way of example, I'll share a story.

I once had a very nice Rottweiler named Otis stay at my home for two weeks of boarding and training while his parents set off on a European vacation. I had known Otis since he was about eight weeks old and you couldn't want a sweeter dog. There wasn't a mean bone in his body and he was completely tolerant of anything the three small children in his household could dish out. So imagine my surprise on Otis' first night at my home when I walked near him while he was eating and he began growling at me. I was totally shocked. After reprimanding him I immediately phoned the owners, hoping to catch them before they left on their trip, to talk to them about this. The first thing I asked was if they fed the dog alone in an isolated area. I knew the answer would be yes and indeed it was. When I informed the owner of what happened he responded with surprise, "Well, he's never done that before."

Of course he hadn't. Nobody had ever come near him while he was eating. Otis always got to eat alone in the garage and everyone was instructed not to disturb him. "What are you going to do if one of your kids accidentally goes near him while he's eating?" I asked. "Uh, well, I guess I don't know," came the reply. Clearly growling at you while eating (or any other time for that matter), is not acceptable behavior and you should work from the moment you realize there's a problem to ensure that your dog will never be protective or aggressive around food or toys of any kind. If you're not sure how your dog will react, now would be a good time to test him.

If you do indeed have a problem, then implement the routine demonstrated in the pictures on the opposing page. Let's begin with the food bowl. Start by walking near the dog while he's eating, but not close enough to elicit a reaction. As you pass him throw a treat in his direction and keep going. After he picks it up and goes back to his dish, repeat the procedure. Keep doing this until your dog anticipates that you're going to throw him a treat each time you enter his "zone" and then start moving closer to him. Still only *pass through* his "zone," that is, walk by, toss him the treat and keep walking. This way he will not feel that his zone is truly being encroached on. You're just passing through and leaving a goodie in your wake. That's not so bad. You'll notice that soon your dog will pick his head up from his bowl as you approach in anticipation of the treat. When this happens, it's time to start moving a little closer to him and then a little closer again and so on. Eventually you'll be standing right next to him tossing treats into or near his dish (depends on your aim) while he's eating. Now it's time to start touching him during his meal. Gently place your hand on his back or side as he's eating and while you're touching him, throw treats into his dish. In the beginning, you might have to throw treats in relatively rapid succession, but as your dog gets habituated to this you can slow down the treat count continually. Eventually, your dog

From outside his reaction zone, toss him treats while he's eating.

As he gets more comfortable with this over time, move closer. But take your time, don't rush it.

Photos: Rose Guilbert

Continue until you can stand next to him and touch him while dropping treats in the dish.

Keep in mind that in real life getting from picture one to picture three could take a few weeks.

will have no problem with you standing near him and touching him while he's having his meal. As long as things are moving along rather well, continue by making your touching of the dog more and more pronounced. In other words, while initially you might have only had your hand resting on your dog's back you should graduate to being able to stroke him across increasing areas of his body for longer and longer periods of time. When you've arrived at this point, your dog should have no further issues with you standing near him and touching him while he's eating. In other words, he's no longer protective over his zone. Once you can do this have other members of the household practice as well until the dog no longer has an issue with people near him while he's eating.

This brings you to the next exercise: actually taking the bowl away from the dog. There are two approaches you can use here, and which one you choose will be a field decision you'll have to make. If you feel that you can safely reach in and grab your dog's dish without creating a response go ahead and do so, place a very yummy treat on top of the dog's food and return it to him. If you don't feel good about this, you'll have to start at a more basic level. Sit on the floor, as demonstrated in the adjacent pictures, with two bowls in your possession: an empty one and one with his meal in it. With the bowls on one side of you and your dog on the other, take a handful of food out of the full dish, place it in the empty one, and hand it to your dog. *Do not let go of the dish!* Continue to hold on to it while the dog is eating, and when he's through pull the dish away and place another handful of food in it. Then, repeat the procedure. This will get your dog used to the idea that your hand is near his dish often and that when your hand removes his dish it will momentarily be returning with more food. In other words, the dish being removed is a prelude to more food, not to losing a valued resource.

Have an empty and full dish on one side, the dog on the other.

Put a handful of kibble in the empty bowl and...

give it to the dog

then repeat until the meal is done.

Photos: Rose Guilbert

When you've arrived at this point you can take the next step. Put several handfuls of food in your dog's dish and begin taking it away from him *before he's finished,* placing a delicious treat on top of it and promptly returning it to him. Gradually let him empty the bowl and then repeat this procedure until he is totally comfortable with it.

Only when your dog is completely habituated to this routine and has no problem with it should you begin actually taking your hand off the food dish, just momentarily, then reaching in again and repeating the procedure. Gradually leave your hand off the dish longer and longer before reaching in to take it again. By the time you get to this point, your dog will have had you take his dish away so many times that it simply won't matter to him. This, of course, is the whole idea. Once you're at this juncture you can bring the two elements of this program together. That is, approach your dog while he's eating, take his dish up, place a treat on top and return it to him. Then, leave the area. A few minutes later repeat the procedure and soon your dog will be very comfortable with you around his food dish.

Once everything looks okay you should add a third element: the "off" command. If you're not sure how to teach this command, refer to the section *Do Not Let the Dog Take Food Without Your Permission* on page 35 in the doggie twelve-step program. If you've done everything right so far, you should be able to walk up to your dog's dish while he's eating, command "off," at which point he should take several steps back from his dish. Then you should pick it up, place several delicious treats in it and return it to him. Practice this once or twice per mealtime until the dog has totally internalized this routine. Again, once your dog is comfortable with all of this be sure to have everyone in the household try it. Of course, the point of all this is to teach him to trust you and anticipate something wonderful when you approach the food dish. This will undermine the need he feels to defend his area and thus solve your problem.

Finally, from here on out, do not allow your dog to stake out special, private zones for eating around your house. Feed him in the busiest places at the busiest times so he gets used to having plenty of commotion during mealtimes.

If your dog is possessive over toys, you'll have to implement a similar routine. If you've been following the doggie twelve-step program you will have removed all toys and objects of possession from the dog (see page 41). The following exercise is a great way to reintroduce valued objects. Begin by taking something the dog really loves, like a big, fat knuckle bone, sit down with him and hand it to him. However, *do not let it go.* Hold on to it while the dog is chewing it so that he never has a full sense of possession over it. Once he's chewed on it, command "off" (see page 35), pull the bone away, give your dog a treat and hand it back so he can continue to chew on it. After a few more moments, repeat the procedure. Each time let the dog chew on the bone a little bit longer than the time before, so he gets into it a little more. Again and again, ask him to "off," take it away, give him a treat and return the object. Keep in mind that at this point you should *never take your hand off the bone.* Again, this prevents the dog from feeling that he has full possession over the object and allows you to teach him what will happen if he releases it: he gets a treat and then gets his toy back. From your dog's standpoint this could be viewed as "doggie investing": give up the principal (his bone) for a brief period of time, receive the interest (the treat), and then get the principal back.

Once your dog understands and is comfortable with this routine, you can go to the next step. Again, allow him to chew on the bone while you're holding it. However, now let go of the bone for just a moment, immediately grab it again, command "off," give him a treat, and return the bone just as you did before. The only difference here is that now you're taking your hand off the bone for a moment. Once that's going well, leave your hand off the bone for a moment longer,

Doggie Investing

From your dog's standpoint, these exercises could be viewed as "doggie investing": give up the principal (his bone) for a brief period of time, receive the interest (the treat), and then get the principal back. Easy money!

and then longer, and then longer, until you can leave your hand off it for even several minutes, then reach in, take it, give him a treat, and return it. When this is going well, it's time to add the last couple of steps. You should now be able to give your dog his bone, get up and walk away, return a few moments later, bend down, have him release it and yes, give him a treat before returning it. The final step involves simply approaching the dog while he's chewing on the object, commanding "off" before reaching in to get it, bending over to pick it up, giving him a treat, and returning it. Once you're here, again have everyone in your household try it and soon your dog will be trustworthy around objects. Remember that you cannot practice these exercises too often and the more exposures your dog experiences over a shorter timeframe the better.

Now, some of you might be wondering why I don't just recommend a straight punitive approach with the dog like a yank on a training collar or even a correction with an electronic collar whenever he gives you trouble around objects of possession. The primary reason is that while this might work if *you* are taking the object from the dog since you're the one dishing out the punishment, your dog will not have the same level of fear or respect for your young child. Thus, while he might tolerate this treatment from you, he most likely will not from a baby, who, as I've said, he'll tend to view as a lower-ranking pack member. Moreover, an approach using strictly force will tend to confirm the dog's worst suspicions: the presence of people around his food dish is bad news. By following the program outlined above, your dog will learn to trust you and others around his food dish and thus his initial motivation for guarding is undermined altogether. He will no longer feel the need to protect since he's learned that most of the time he not only gets his object back, he gets a treat to boot. Even when you're no longer using treats to do this, the dog will have been so conditioned to the new routine that the old problem simply won't show up anymore.

Change His Mind Before You Change His Body!

A strictly compulsive approach to object guarding will tend to confirm your dog's worst suspicion: the presence of people around his food dish is bad news. By following this program, your dog will learn to trust you and others around his food dish and thus his initial motivation for guarding is undermined altogether.

WHAT IF MY DOG BARKS EXCESSIVELY?

Barking dogs are annoying enough, but if you have a new-born in the house this habit will surely drive you crazy. During the early stages of motherhood the level of sleep deprivation is notorious. If you add a barking dog who will sporadically wake you and your child at those precious few moments of sleep into that mix, you'll quickly have a very frustrating situation on your hands. It's important that any barking problems be handled long before your child arrives because, frankly, after the baby's born you may not have the patience or the energy for it.

Before we start, it's important to note that barking is a perfectly natural canine behavior and the elimination of all barking is neither feasible nor sensible. However, you should be able to limit your dog's barking to times and places where it's appropriate and doesn't create a problem for anyone. There are any number of situations that will cause your dog to bark, but whatever the case you basically have two choices in how to respond. The first is teaching the dog a "quiet" command and the second is the use of a barking collar. Which you choose depends on your situation and often people will use both. Teaching the dog the command "quiet" is a rather simple and straightforward affair. Take a squirt bottle that has a fairly powerful and direct stream, and fill it either with water or the taste deterrent Bitter Apple™ (for some dogs shake cans work better, so substitute shake can for the squirt bottle if necessary). Try to have this on your person whenever possible (I usually hook the trigger in my pants pocket and carry it around with me like a pistol). This will enable you to reprimand your dog the moment he starts barking rather than having to go looking for the bottle at key moments. If the dog predictably barks only in certain locations such as the front door or window, try to have the bottle permanently placed there for easy retrieval. When your dog begins to bark at whatever it is and you've had enough simply

"Noise, Noise, I Can't Stand the Noise"

Barking dogs and snoozing babies make for a volatile combination in an already sleep-deprived environment that can lead to explosive fits of temper and an eviction notice for your dog. Curbing excessive barking prior to baby's arrival will let everyone sleep more peacefully.

go up to him and command "quiet," wait a moment and then squirt him right in the nose and mouth. *It's important to wait a moment between the bark and the squirt so that the dog has the opportunity to comply.* Of course, in the beginning he won't know what "quiet" means, so inevitably he'll get squirted, but as time goes on he'll learn to identify the word "quiet" as a warning and begin to respond with silence. If the dog resumes barking within the next minute or two, then you may simply squirt him at the same moment that you say "quiet" since at this point it's a reprimand rather than an instruction. In other words, you want him to understand that once you say "quiet" it means he shouldn't bark for a while, and not just give your three seconds of silence. Also, be sure to be sneaky with your bottle, pulling it from behind your back or out of your pocket for just a second, squirting him and then hiding the bottle from his view. You don't want him to learn that "quiet" only has meaning when you've got a bottle around. Rather, you'd like him to believe that you potentially have that thing on you at all times. In other words, you want him to learn that the variable is the word "quiet" and not the squirt bottle. For those dogs that figure out that your bottle's range is limited to a few feet I recommend letting the dog drag a leash around the house for a few days while you're working on this. This way if he attempts to make a run for it you can simply step on the leash and still reprimand him. Crude but effective!

Courtesy: Katie Bracco

This is the basic routine for establishing the word "quiet" as part of your dog's vocabulary. Now let's take a quick look at a few permutations of this exercise that should help you meet the needs of a variety of situations. One thing you eventually want the dog to learn is to obey your "quiet" command from a distance. In other words, you don't want him to keep barking until you can get to him and threaten him with a squirt from the bottle. The key is to teach the dog that he only gets one opportunity to refrain from barking before something unpleasant happens. In the beginning, if you hear your dog barking on the other side of the house *don't say a word*. Let him bark but begin rapidly moving in his direction. Only when you are within squirting range do you issue the command "quiet" just once and then squirt him. Doing this will avoid teaching your dog to ignore your commands until you're right next to him. Instead, it will begin to condition him to respond to "quiet" the first time around. Once he is responding relatively reliably to the "quiet" command when you're nearby, you can go to the next step. Follow exactly the same routine, but this time issue your command from several feet further out. If your dog issues another bark, quickly leap to his side and squirt him. Once he's good from the new distance, add in a little more and then a little more and soon you'll find that your dog will respond to the command "quiet" no matter from where you issue it in the house. Should he decide to test you at some point (most dogs will) by continuing to bark after you've commanded "quiet" when you're a ways away then immediately shout "no" repeatedly as you run into the room where he's barking and then spray him. Continuing to shout the reprimand "no" at him until you reach him ties the squirt he gets from you back to the initial infraction and thus allows you to reprimand him after the fact. If your dog is one of those that will keep barking until you appear and then suddenly quiet down, squirt him anyway. Teach him that once he's blown off your initial "quiet" command, it's too late, he's doomed. Using this approach you'll soon have a dog that responds to your "quiet" command with silence. That means that in any given situation you have the choice whether to allow your dog to bark or

There are a variety of anti-barking collars available to silence canis interruptus and which you choose, should you need one, will be determined by the tenacity and temperament of your dog. Fortunately, most of them work quickly and effectively with minimal discomfort to your dog.

not. This is important because there are circumstances during which you might want your dog to bark, such as when an encyclopedia salesman knocks on your door or the pizza guy brings the wrong pizza.

Now, there might be times when you are neither in the mood nor in the position to command the dog to be quiet. For instance, if your baby just went to sleep, telling your dog to be quiet after he starts barking would almost be pointless since the damage is already done. Both you and your child are now awake. For situations like this, and others where you simply want the dog to be quiet without any instruction from you I recommend anti-barking collars. Of these there are two varieties: citronella spray collars and electronic collars (actually, there are others, such as collars that emit annoying sounds that supposedly only your dog can hear but I have found them to be by and large ineffective). My first choice is always the citronella spray collar because it is pain free and utterly harmless. It simply sprays the dog under the muzzle with citronella spray, derived from a citrus-based essential oil, which smells good to humans and horrible to dogs. The dog barks, he gets sprayed. It's that simple. The timing is perfect every time and you don't have to be there. Your dog quickly learns that when he has the collar on, barking is unacceptable and he'll maintain silence when wearing the collar. End of problem! If you want to take a nap with your baby, fit the dog with the collar and go to sleep.

For about eighty-five percent of dogs, citronella collars are supremely effective. However, there are those hard cases who will either be unaffected by the collar or figure out that if they bark about fifteen to twenty times they will empty the collar and then they're home free. For these dogs, I recommend electronic collars. Some people might find this harsh, but I assure you the dog will not be getting corrected very often. As with the citronella collar, the dog will quickly learn that wearing the collar demands silence and after learning this he will shortly stop testing the collar. In other words, the number of corrections experienced by the dog from either collar is usually relatively low. When buying an electronic collar, I recommend ones that allow you to set different stimulation levels for the varying sensitivities of dogs. That way you can find that level that's just enough to get the job done without hurting your dog and minimize the level of discomfort your dog has to experience in order to be silent. In either case, the barking problem usually comes to an end in short order.

The good news about barking collars is that in many situations you won't have to use them very long: perhaps only six to eight weeks – maybe even less. That's because often the dog will learn to identify a particular situation with the need for silence. This is called *situational learning* and can work both for and against you. In this case, it works for you. Consider the following example. One of the peculiarities of my own life is that I run a meditation center out of my home. That means that between 7:30 and 8:30 every evening I need silence in the house. I can't very well have a dog in the other room barking while people are trying to meditate, I mean, being the big dog trainer and all. So, the moment I realized I had a problem I put a citronella collar on my dog and the barking evaporated. Interestingly, what I found was that after about a month of wearing the collar she no longer needed it. She'd learned that particular time frame and that location demanded silence and she simply got conditioned to it. It's been four and a half years since then and I've never had another problem with her. The same was true with barking in the car if she'd been left in there for a while. A month of the citronella collar and I haven't heard a peep from her since.

All that having been said, let's talk briefly about teaching the dog a new set of responses to certain stimuli that cause barking. You may or may not find this necessary in your given situation but it's nice to have the information. The classic example of a conditioned barking response is the dog that always barks at the sound of the doorbell. Wouldn't it be nice if, when your dog heard the doorbell ring, instead of running to the door barking like crazy, he ran to you and sat at your feet with rapt attention? Training your dog to do this is easier than you think. I recently had a client with one of the most chronic barkers I'd ever met who taught her dog to do this in about a week and a half. Begin by having someone stand outside your door and ring the bell. You're standing inside the door armed with a squirt bottle and each time your dog barks he gets sprayed. You're teaching him, "No barking at the door, period." It might take some time to totally squelch the bark response in your dog since the barking is so powerfully conditioned in him at this point that he literally cannot help himself. But eventually you'll see that your dog will make a choice not to bark. *The moment he does you immediately reward him with a treat.* The next time the doorbell rings, if he barks, he gets sprayed, if he inhibits himself, he gets a treat. Soon the weight and momentum of his conditioning are going to shift to being quiet and getting a treat. Getting to this point on a consistent basis may take a few days, but it will definitely happen. The job now is to powerfully condition the dog to expect a treat from you each time he hears the door-bell. You can accelerate this process by tape recording about a minute's worth of doorbell rings and playing them back to your dog throughout the day. Each time he hears the taped bell ring, guess what? He gets a treat. Once he's on to you, try setting it up so the dog hears the tape recorder ring at some distance from you. Once it rings, encourage him to come to you to get his treat. Soon you'll find that when he hears the doorbell ring, rather than rushing the door in a barking frenzy, he will come looking to you for his treat – "presto, chango", you have a new dog!

I want to cover couple of final observations about barking. Sometimes the best solutions are the easiest ones and are thus overlooked. For instance, if your dog barks because he's running around in the backyard chasing cats or squirrels or he's hanging around the front window going off at every

Pavlov's Door

Rather than running to the door barking like a lunatic every time someone comes to the house, teach your dog to come to you when someone is at the door and offer you his undivided attention. Through the incredible power of conditioning it's easier than you think.

passerby the simplest solution might be to deny him access to these areas. Rather than being in the backyard or by the front window when you need some silence, perhaps he should be in his crate or a quiet part of the house chewing on a favorite bone. Also, be aware that often barking is a boredom related behavior. The dog is barking because there simply isn't anything else to do and, let's face it, barking is fun. Getting the dog more exercise and playtime after which he comes home exhausted would be very helpful.

At any rate, an intelligent combination of the suggestions outlined above should help you eliminate any barking problems before your child arrives. Doing so will give you peace of mind and allow you to put your energy where it should be: with your baby.

WHAT IF MY DOG IS OVERLY PROTECTIVE?

If your dog is overly protective in relation to you, there's a high likelihood that he'll express the same behavior in relation to your child. In other words, he might inappropriately "protect" your child against someone who has every right to be there. "How could a dog be *overly* protective?" you might wonder. Isn't it good that he's protective? Well, actually, no! Not if his suspicions are leading him to draw the wrong conclusions. If your dog has bitten or threatened to bite in this context please read the section entitled *Dealing with the Serious Problem Dog* on page 92. If you feel that your dog is borderline and has the potential to become a problem, read on.

The first thing to do with a dog like this is to be sure that you're completely following the "Doggie Twelve-Step Program" outlined above (see page 17). The reason is that overly protective dogs are often operating under the assumption that they're the leader of the pack. That is, part of the pack leader's job is to protect its members. Thus, in many cases when dogs are acting inappropriately protective it's because they feel responsible *for* their owners rather than *to* their

Too Much of a Good Thing

*While all of us would like our dogs to feel protective over us, this can be a mixed blessing. Be sure your dog feels responsible **to you** rather than **for you**. A dog that feels responsible to you will look to you for guidance and direction in all things. That means you'll be able to help him make decisions. A dog that feels responsible for you will make his own decisions, decisions which are usually inappropriate, sometimes dangerous and can land you in a world of trouble.*

owners. This is a critical difference. In many cases you'll find that once the dog is effectively put on a rank management program the problematic outbursts of threats or aggression simply cease or are at least significantly diminished. If not, then it's usually a relatively simple matter to make them disappear.

You can begin by keeping your dog on a leash with you or on a tie down, thus restricting his ability to control his perimeter

Courtesy: Candyce Plummer Gaudiani Photography

and act out inappropriately outside your zone of influence. If he begins to act out with any lunging or barking, simply squirt him with the Bitter Apple™ spray, rattle a shake can, or give him a correction on his collar. It is important for him to know that you, his leader, seriously disapprove of this behavior. Once he's inhibiting himself, redirect his energy by giving him obedience commands. This shouldn't pose a problem since theoretically you've already trained the com- mands in the context of the rank management program. *Once the dog is controlled and no longer reactive*, have the "intruders" begin tossing treats to him from a safe zone, an area where they don't have to worry about your dog going after them. Be sure to instruct these people not to attempt to solicit an interaction from your dog as this can make him apprehensive and thus reac- tive. Just have them continue to throw treats to him so long as he's behaving and otherwise ignore him. If it appears that your dog would like to seek out an interaction with your guest, by all means, let him. But continue to instruct your guest to be relatively aloof with your dog and physically engage him only to the degree that your dog is willing to entertain such an engagement.

Repeating this procedure as often as possible and in as many different contexts as possible will begin to change your dog's response to these situations and eventually he will come to understand that anyone you allow into your home or proximity should not only be okay with him but could be the source of something nice as well.

To fully implement this change of heart, especially if your dog has been suspicious for a long time, may take awhile and there may be ups and downs. But, as with everything else, if you start as soon as possible and work as diligently as possible, you should be able to overcome this problem within three to six weeks.

WHAT IF I HAVE SEVERAL DOGS AND THEY DON'T GET ALONG WELL TOGETHER?

In behavioral lingo this is referred to as *sibling rivalry*. If your dogs are experiencing a great deal of tension in relation to one another, you should consider this a major red flag, since many dogs tend to view children as lower ranking pack members and will thus potentially treat them similarly. That is, pack members that are perceived to be getting out of line are corrected, usually with a bite. If your dogs have bitten or threatened to bite each other or you in this context please read the section entitled *Dealing with the Serious Problem Dog* on page 92.

If your dogs are simply tense, moody, or jealous around one another there are a few things you can do to straighten out the situation. First, implement the rank management program outlined above and *ensure that both of your dogs unequivocally view you as their leader*. As pack leader, you have the right to control conflict in your group, a right you may have to exercise. Also, try to assess which of your dogs is higher ranking and which is lower ranking. If you're not sure, ask yourself questions such as: does one dog occasionally prevent the other from entering the room? Does one dog habitually demand another get out of his way? Does one dog proudly parade a toy around in front of the other taunting him with it but refusing to let him get it? Which dog goes out the door first if both have equal opportunity? Can one dog

Domestic Violence

Do you have several dogs in the house that seem to suffer from irreconcilable differences? If so you'd better jump in headlong to help them resolve their issues or, with a new pack member on the way, an ugly divorce might be inevitable. A firm and guided mediation is what's called for and you'd better play the mediator.

force the other to leave the room or drop a toy with a simple look and some posturing? Closely observing the relationship between your dogs should help you figure out which one is higher ranking and which one is lower ranking.

Having figured this out, you must be sure to reinforce the dominant dog in his position and simultaneously remind the lower ranking dog of his subordinate status. Failing to do so is a leading cause of serious trouble between dogs in the same home. Dogs have a whole host of behaviors they display in relation to one another, (such as those implied by the questions just mentioned) and they use them to work out their relationship. But often a person enters the picture and unknowingly sends the dogs signals that might imply the exact opposite of what they've worked out. The most common reason for this is that people feel sorry for the underdog and start giving him special treatment. This, of course, totally annoys the more dominant dog who'll be sure to go out of his way to put the other one in his place the first opportunity he gets. Having a situation go back and forth like this can build unresolved tension between the dogs that can often explode into cases of extreme and even deadly aggression. Dogs that relate to each other this way will quite possibly relate to your child in the same manner. Therefore, it's extremely important that once you figure out who's higher ranking, you reinforce the positions that they've worked out between each other. This means that you actually treat the more dominant dog preferentially by giving him a little more affection, the better treats, the more desirable resting places, etc. and you do it *in such a way that both dogs are aware of it.* Moreover, you also reprimand the lower ranking dog for any dominant overtures towards the higher ranking dog. Implementing this standard, difficult as it might be to our egalitarian sensibilities, ensures that all the social signals flowing to the dogs from every aspect of their environment are consistent with what they've worked out between each other. In this way no residual tension will develop between and there will be nothing for them to fight over. Remember, while in the human world

A Sound Bite

Remember, while in the human world equality might equal justice, in the canine world equality equals violence.

equality might equal justice, in the canine world equality equals violence. Be sure to be the leader of your pack and then understand and enforce its hierarchy.

WHAT IF MY DOG HAS KILLED OR SERIOUSLY INJURED DOMESTIC ANIMALS

The killing of domestic animals, whether yours or other people's, is a serious red flag. Usually such behavior is driven by predatory instincts and is extremely difficult to resolve *reliably*. Because of the level of force involved, having such a dog around a small child is an extremely questionable undertaking. Children have shrill, high-pitched, voices and move in erratic and unpredictable ways. These are just the kind of actions that can trigger predatory responses in a dog. Each year, numerous fatalities of small children due to dog attacks are reported. A great many of those are perpetrated by the family dog and often prey motivation was the culprit. In a number of cases the dog actually went up to the infant's crib, pulled it out, and killed it. If you have a dog that has killed or seriously injured a domestic animal I would strongly recommend re-homing the dog as soon as possible. For more on this, please read the section below entitled *Dealing with the Serious Problem Dog*.

IN CLOSING

It takes time to resolve problem behaviors, so the sooner you start working on any issues you have with your dog the better. But even if it's rather late in the day and you're about to have your baby anytime, or have already had it, there may still be time. A great many of the above mentioned issues don't become real problems until your child is about eight months old. It's at this age that most kids begin crawling and walking and thus the encounters between your dog and your child are guaranteed to be more frequent and less predictable. It's during these interactions that you'll find out whether or not you've done the work you need to, so please use the time before that wisely!

Tired Dogs are Good Dogs!

I've said it a few times throughout this book and I'm saying it again because of its extreme importance. An overwhelming percentage of behavior problems in dogs could be eliminated or at least diminished with adequate exercise. So much of what creates problems for people with their dogs is simply boredom related. If you're not in a position to give your dog the exercise he needs find someone who can. An entire industry of pet care professionals has evolved in the last decade to help you deal with precisely this issue. Also, ten or fifteen minutes of tight obedience routines that your dog finds challenging and stimulating can be the equivalent of at least the same time spent exercising. Whatever amount of energy you can drain out of your dog through exercise will be energy that he doesn't have available to get himself into trouble. So do both of you a favor and give him a workout.

DEALING WITH THE SERIOUS PROBLEM DOG

 In several of the above discussions I've directed the reader to this section if the dog has actually bitten or come very close to biting a person. That is not because the behavior modification routines outlined above wouldn't work for such dogs—they will—but because when a child is involved, cases involving the possibility of real aggression need special consideration.

A Difficult Decision

Perhaps the hardest decision some people have to make is whether or not keeping their current dog with a history of aggression is appropriate given the arrival of a child.

The main consideration, of course, is whether or not it's appropriate to have this dog in the presence of a child. Assessing this question is more art than science but there are four factors I usually consider when someone approaches me with this situation: threshold of reactivity; level of intensity; previous history; and crossover considerations.

By *threshold of reactivity*, I mean how much of a certain type of stimulation is necessary in order to make the dog reactive, or act out in ways that are undesirable. By *level of intensity*, I mean once the threshold of reactivity is crossed how intense is the response. Does it involve just a bark and an effort to retreat or is there a lashing out aggressively including biting. If there is biting, how severe is it? Is it a nip with the front of the mouth or a full on bite with the middle or back of the mouth? Then there's *previous history*. How long is your dog's history for this kind of behavior? What kind of rap sheet does he have? Of course, the longer the history, the more powerful the momentum behind the behavior and thus the greater the cause for concern. Finally, there is a *crossover consideration*. In other words, let's say your dog is possessive around the food dish, but has never done more than issue a slight growl when you approach him, but he's also been in dog fights where he's seriously injured another dog. I would consider this a huge red flag because, though the dog's reactivity and level of intensity around the food dish is moderate, his level of intensity in relation to another dog is very high. My concern would be that in relation to a child—whom your dog might view as a lower ranking pack member—he would use the same level of intensity that he has previously used against other dogs, and thus present a serious threat.

If your dog is having behavior problems that potentially involve a severely aggressive response, you should consider whether or not you can responsibly keep this dog in the presence of a new child. Most of these problems are totally reversible and manageable, and if a child weren't involved I would most definitely argue for working with them. However, with a child the risks are too great (for both child and dog—for if your dog ends up biting your child, you're going to be faced with not only potentially serious injuries, but also some very tough choices about the life of your dog). In cases like this, I would urge you to consider re-homing your dog.

If you feel very strongly about keeping the dog, my advice is to immediately seek the help of a qualified behavior professional. Finding such a person can be difficult, but there are a few things to look for. Ask around at the veterinary offices in your area for recommendations. Also, ask at the dog park and in your neighborhood. If the same name comes up again and again, this is a person you might check with. I would suggest avoiding trainers whose primary solution to every behavior problem is a yank on the choke chain. Such a one-dimensional and strictly compulsive approach is a clear indication that this person is not really familiar with serious behavior issues. I'm not suggesting that you should avoid trainers who use compulsive methods for sometimes, when intelligently applied, these are indispensable in modifying problem behaviors. But whoever you find should at least be fluent with the principles outlined in this book and have a thorough working knowledge of both fear-based and rank-based aggression problems and their resolution. They should be able to speak with you intelligently about such topics as systematic desensitization, counter-conditioning, and rank management and should be willing to explain these concepts

An Ounce of Prevention

If your dog is having behavior problems that potentially involve a severely aggressive response, you should consider whether or not you can responsibly keep this dog in the presence of a new child. Most of these problems are totally reversible and manageable, and if a child weren't involved I would most definitely argue for working with them. However, with a child the risks are too great (for both child and dog—for if your dog ends up biting your child, you're going to be faced with not only potentially serious injuries, but also some very tough choices about the life of your dog). In cases like this, I would urge you to consider re-homing your dog.

to you until you understand them. After all, you're the person who's going to have to implement these programs.

Also, avoid trainers who promise you across the board that they can fix all behavior problems if you just spend enough money with them. A good trainer will not only understand his own limitations, but also the limitations of the situation, and should be very frank with you about them. And finally, in relation to resolving the specific behavior issues discussed above, I would hesitate sending the dog away for training. A great many of these issues are directly related to the relationship you have with your dog and thus you should work on them in the context of your life as it is. The only time sending him away for training under these circumstances might make sense would be with the understanding that that is a beginning and that you'd be committed to continuing the work your trainer has started during your dog's period away.

Now if you've found a trainer/behaviorist who appears competent and who's worked with your dog for some time and he or she suggests that you re-home your dog I would strongly recommend taking their advice. No matter how you feel about your dog, you cannot put your new child at risk because in the end it's both the child and the dog who will pay the price. Finding him a new home without a child now will ensure that everyone lives happily ever after later.

A Seamless Transition

 The most critical element in making the arrival of your new child as seamless and easy as possible is to introduce as many of the changes that this arrival will certainly entail as soon as possible. This way, your dog will not associate these changes with the arrival of the baby and thus won't have a reason to take a dim view of the newcomer. If prepared for properly, the arrival of your baby from the perspective of the dog will appear to be a mere hiccup in his routine. In an ideal world, the new elements of his routine would be introduced at least three to four months before the delivery date.

Photos: Rose Guilbert

In order to prepare for this, begin by thinking about what your house rules are going to be once you have a child and start implementing those rules today. If you no longer want your dog on the bed, get him off now (see page 20). If you don't want him on the furniture, same thing (see page 20). If you don't want him begging at the table, stop the behavior now (see page 35). If he's a counter surfer, deal with it today (see page 35). If he's going to have to be isolated for periods of time during the day, begin introducing such isolation now (page 64). If you've skipped over the Doggie Twelve-Step Program you might glance at it to see if there are any behaviors you haven't thought of that you might want to curb with your dog. The long and the short of it is: start today what you'll need to do tomorrow and tomorrow is less likely to be filled with trouble.

Dogs, Children, and Toys

In addition to these issues there are a few others to think about as well. One has to do with toys. If your dog is possessive over objects, (see page 73) You might have noticed that a great many dog toys bear a striking similarity to children's toys. If you don't want your dog to appropriate every toy that comes into the house help him differentiate what's his from what's not his now. There are several ways to accomplish this. First, try to avoid buying toys for your dog that are too much like kid's toys. My favorite dog toys are easily identifiable as such, for example, tennis balls, hard rubber toys that allow you to put food in them such as Kong Toys™, Planet Toys™, Buster Cubes or Balls™, hollow bones with marrow holes that can be stuffed with food, corn starch bones, and so on. Second, don't have a million dog toys lying around. Let your dog have access to only two or three that are easily identifiable. Even if you've found eight or ten toys that your dog really likes, rotate them so they're not always scattered about the house. The more of his things he's used to having scattered around, the higher the likelihood that he's going to assume that anything lying around on the floor is his.

Finally, you can teach him to discriminate between his toys and children's toys by taking advantage of his powerful sense of smell. To do this, begin practicing the simple exercise outlined below. Start with two piles of toys, one a child's pile, one a dog's pile, separated by a few feet. On the toys in the child's pile put a dab of diluted Listerine™ so the dog can begin to build a scent association with these toys. Then, every time your dog approaches the child's pile command "off" (see page 35 if your dog doesn't know "off"). If he approaches his own pile praise him. Try this at different times of the day in different parts of the house with different groups of toys. Once he's good at this exercise begin moving the piles closer and closer together until they're right next to each other. Continue to use the "off" command if he even thinks about picking up a child's toy. Once he's really good at this it's time to increase the difficulty quotient. Mix the toys in the two piles together. Once again, if he shows interest in the child's toys it's an "off" command and if he goes for his own toys he's a good boy. Continue to practice this exercise throughout your pregnancy. Each time you buy a new child's toy put a dab of diluted Listerine™ on it, show it to the dog while commanding "off" and then add it to your steadily growing collection of toys. Your dog will soon figure out what's his and what isn't and so long as you keep his own toy pile interesting, especially by stuffing some items with food, you shouldn't have any trouble.

THE CHILD'S ROOM AND OTHER ZONES

Something else to think about is creating certain zones in the house to which the dog will have limited access. For instance, the child's new room, areas where you're planning to nurse your child, the space around his high chair, and finally, the space around the baby himself are all places in which the dog should be conditioned to follow certain rules. Let's go down this list and see what you can do to define these zones.

Canine Rules of Possession

What's mine is mine and what's yours is mine is a dog's general theory of ownership unless otherwise instructed. The following list of dog property laws, gleaned from the Internet, pretty well sums it up.

1. If I like it, it's mine.
2. If it's in my mouth, it's mine.
3. If I can take it from you, it's mine.
4. If I had it a little while ago, it's mine.
5. If it's mine, it must never appear to be yours in any way.
6. If I'm chewing something up, all the pieces are mine.
7. If it just looks like mine, it's mine.
8. If I saw it first, it's mine.
9. If you are playing with something and you put it down, it automatically becomes mine.
10. If it's broken, it's yours.

Simplify your dog's life by
1. teaching him that everything is yours and
2. getting him toys that he can easily distinguish from your child's toys and teaching him the difference between the two.

The Zone Defense

Teaching your dog to respect certain zones around our child will build a huge safety margin into their relationship. It will also give you great latitude in controlling your dog's interactions with your child and using them to cultivate both propriety and a positive outlook on the whole situation.

In my view, the child's room should be an area to which the dog only has access with your permission. You want him to understand that this is not a playground, a resting area, or an area in any way available to him unless he has your okay. This will not only build in a necessary safeguard, it will also allow you to teach him to build positive associations with this room and thus with your child – but more on that in a moment. Right now, let's talk about teaching him that he's never to enter this room without your permission. I'll run down a number of methods you can use and I suggest working with them all just to ensure that your dog really gets it. Begin by having the dog on a leash with a training collar (pinch collars are preferable over choke chains – see the appendix for a discussion of collars). Then, walk him near the baby's future room and begin throwing treats on the ground *on the outside of the room*, allowing the dog to get them. Throw six to eight treats down until your dog is really into it and then suddenly toss the next one into the child's room. Most dogs will charge right towards the room and as he approaches the threshold of the door give him a quick nudge on the collar combined with a sharp "no." The level of force you use should be tempered to the sensitivity of your dog. You should find the level that's just enough to get the job done the first time around. Anything more is abusive and anything less is as well, since you'll merely have to give the correction more often. Of course, after this happens the first time your dog will be somewhat surprised and try to figure out why he got corrected. To help him out continue to throw more treats on the ground *on your side of the door* and encourage him to get them (I'll explain this in a minute). After he's had enough treats to get him excited once more, toss another one into the room and repeat the correction. As soon as your dog has been corrected, once again start throwing him treats on your side of the door. What you're doing is playing a game I call "identify the variable." You want him to figure out what the difference is between the treats on your side of the door and on the other side, and of course, it's the door that's the difference. It's important to bring the dog back to taking treats on your side of the door as soon as possible after his correction in order to both bring his attitude up and teach him that it's not the treats themselves that are the problem. You'll be amazed at how fast most dogs pick this up. Usually three to five repetitions and the dog starts getting it. Now, the first time you throw a treat into the room and the dog hesitates to go in, you should *immediately praise him wildly* and offer him a treat from your hand. You want to highlight for him the moment he got it right not simply through the lack of a correction, but through a positive consequence as well.

Once your dog gets this, you should make things a bit more complicated for him. If he has a favorite toy like a tennis ball that he likes to chase, give him a few throws near the baby's room and then suddenly throw one right into the room. Again, if he attempts to go in the room to retrieve the toy, he gets a correction and if he refuses to enter he gets wildly praised and perhaps even a treat. Once your dog understands these exercises try periodically walking him past the baby's room and suddenly, outside of what he can identify as a training situation and without warning, throw a treat or a favorite toy into the room. At this point, if he attempts to enter the room, a sharp verbal command should do the trick and thus you should be able to do this without a leash. If you can't, then you should go back to the first stages of the exercise until a verbal reprimand is all you need. Ultimately you should need no reprimand whatsoever since your dog will have learned never to go into that room.

Courtesy: Bari Halperin

When your dog has thoroughly understood this exercise you can work the entire concept from a new angle. Of course, the more angles from which you work this the more solid your dog's understanding will be of what you're trying to teach him. With your dog on the outside of the room, put a few favorite family members or friends inside the room. Once the dog knows they're there, have them do anything they can to entice the dog to come into the room, *aside from actually calling him to come.* They should make high pitched squeaky sounds, toss his favorite toy around inside the room, look at him, tell him what a good boy he is and generally attempt to be as interesting as possible to him. You should be in the room also and if your dog attempts to cross the threshold of the door immediately verbally reprimand him and give him a quick squirt in the nose with Bitter Apple™ spray. Now this may seem inherently unfair but remember, you're trying to teach him that no matter what it looks like he's simply not allowed in that room, period. Keep in mind, one day your child might be rolling around on the floor laughing and looking like a perfect playmate for your dog. Won't it be nice to know that your dog would never go in there unless you give him permission?

A final exercise that will really nail this behavior down involves the use of a Scat-Mat™, a rubber mat with a harmless yet annoying static pulse running through it. Lay this mat down right in front of the door to the child's room and turn it on. This is ideal if your dog is the type that will attempt to go into the room as soon as you're not in the area. The moment he steps on the mat he'll get a surprising static pulse on his feet and will quickly learn to avoid the area. You can also tempt the dog to cross into the area as in the exercises described above. A couple of steps onto the mat will convince him that this is a bad idea. Once the dog gets this, be sure to leave the mat outside the door for at least a few weeks. Soon your dog will stop thinking of that room as a place that he can enter and most of your training goals will have been accomplished. You'll soon find that you can dispose with the Scat-Mat™

There is, however, one more thing. *The idea here is not that the dog should never enter the room, it's that he should learn never to enter that room without your permission.* When he's really understood the first part (at least a few weeks should have gone by during which he hasn't attempted to enter the room and he's passed all your tests) you can teach him the second one also. If you're using a Scat-Mat™ simply turn it off, invite the dog into the room with a command such as "come on in" and then encourage him to enter. He may hesitate in the beginning but continue to encourage him, even gently with the leash and a few treats, if necessary, until he comes along. When he walks across and nothing unpleasant happens, he'll begin to realize that it's safe to enter the room *so long as you're with him and have given him specific permission.* Even if you're not using the Scat-Mat™, the same principle applies. That is, he learns that once you've given the okay, and only then, nothing unpleasant happens if he enters the room. As you will see in the next section, this will come in very handy when you try to make the baby room into a special place with which he has all sorts of positive associations.

Once your dog will enter the baby room only with your okay you can add another element. After bringing him into the room, have him do obedience exercises for you there. Teach him to associate this context with taking direction from you. Never let him get the sense that this is a free-for-all play area. In particular, it would be a good idea to have a special place, like a dog bed, in the room on which he'd learn to spend a good bit of time on a down-stay. Teach him to associate this room with controlled behavior now and once your child arrives such behavior will be second nature to him.

Having defined the baby's room as a special zone, think about other areas where the same controlled behavior would be useful and begin to define those as special zones now. Areas where you think you'll be nursing your child would fall into this category. So would the child's high chair. Defining certain areas as special zones is not particularly difficult but, as with

Entrapment!

In attempting to change a dog's behavior most trainers will resort to the use of "set-ups," creating situations that will almost certainly tempt your dog to do precisely what it is you don't want him to do. While this may seem inherently unfair, it really isn't. Rather, it's a quick way to teach him that no matter what it looks like, a certain behavior is unacceptable. It also puts you in the position of giving him consistent and well-timed feedback about what's okay and what isn't leading to behavioral changes very quickly.

everything else, a little diligence and persistence are required. As with the boundary training for the child's room, set-ups are the key. Identify the zone you'd like to outline and begin using your squirt bottle and the command "out" to enforce its boundaries. Every time your dog enters the area (generally a five to six foot circle around the object) in a firm tone command "out." If the dog does not immediately leave the area he gets a quick squirt from either the water bottle or the now hated Bitter Apple™ spray. A few repetitions of this should give him the idea and he should be especially responsive if you've done all or most of the other things outlined in this book so far. In other words, he'll be so receptive to taking direction from you that at this point a little should go a long way.

When your child is very young you'll want to define the areas where you nurse in this manner, but as he gets older his high chair will become his central feeding place. While, as we'll see shortly, it would be all right to invite the dog to enter the zone and calmly lie next to you when you're nursing, once your child starts using a high chair I would recommend never to let your dog into the eating zone. That's because little children are notoriously messy eaters and once they're in a high chair, there will be food flying in all directions. This will only get worse as your child gets older. If your dog is in the eating zone he'll quickly learn that the child's eating area is a great place for table scraps. "So what?" you might say to yourself. "If the dog eats the mess I won't have to clean it up." That might be true, but I'd prefer if your dog didn't view your child as a source of food. It won't take a huge stretch of your dog's imagination for him to continue to view your child in this way. Once junior becomes more mobile and starts crawling and then running around the house with cookies in hand, it'll be very tempting for your dog to resort to highway robbery by stealing things from him. From there, it's not a long way for him to see this obviously helpless and uncoordinated little child as a lower-ranking pack member and a source of food. A

Situational Learning

As stated previously, situational learning can work both for you and against you. In this case it will work for as your dog begins to associate situations in which your child is present with acceptable and positive behaviors.

competitive dynamic may be set in motion that can be the source of serious behavior problems. You can avoid all of this by simply teaching the dog to respect the child's eating zones exactly in the way he should respect yours.

THE STROLLER

Soon a stroller is going to become a semi-permanent feature of you and your dog's lives. Therefore, you might as well begin introducing it now. Not only do you want your dog to be familiar with the stroller visually, you want him to learn how to walk next to it without pulling or lunging. A dog that lunges and pulls on the leash while you're trying to walk your child in its stroller is dangerous and will have to stay home. Of course, the foundation of proper leash behavior is the exercise entitled "the pay attention game" described on page 27. Before you can even think about taking a dog out with your child in the stroller, this exercise must be mastered. Once this is well in hand, the rest is a piece of cake.

Simply prepare your dog to walk calmly next to the stroller by taking him out with it as much as possible before your due date. Since in this situation you won't be in a position to do the sudden turnarounds described in the training exercise in the chapter discussing rank management, simple nudges on the leash will have to do. Since your stroller is empty you won't have to worry about endangering your baby while working with your dog. As you're walking with your dog and stroller, try to teach the dog to maintain a position in an imaginary box next to it. It doesn't matter which side you pick, as long as you consistently stick to that side. If your dog steps outside the imaginary box you should give a quick leash nudge accompanied by some kind of verbal reprimand such as "no" or "ah, ah, ah." Once he's in the box you should teach him to associate that position with a word or phrase such as "with me," and something positive like an occasional treat. If

Head Collars

There are some dogs who, despite your work with the "pay attention game" (page 27), will still pull ahead slightly when out with the stroller and who respond to nudges on the leash by backing up for three seconds and then forging out again. In this case I will occasionally recommend one of the variety of head collars such as Halti's™ and Gentle Leaders™ that are available today. While I generally do not like these collars for a variety of reasons this is a situation where one might be useful. If you decide to use a head collar please be sure never to snap the lead but rather to gently pull the dog back. Also be sure to carefully read the instructions and perhaps even get some help in learning how to use it.

your dog learns that good things happen to him inside the box he's likely to want to hang around in there. Some people like to use the word "heel," which is fine, though I don't generally use it in this context since true heeling is a precision exercise that requires enormous attention from both dog and owner. Whatever phrase you use, once you've said it enough times and rewarded the dog while he is in the right position, he will associate positive experiences with that position and easily fall into it. *Once you feel that he understands this concept* you should hold him responsible to it by giving him a leash nudge if he fails to comply after he's heard your "with me" command. What you'll find is that soon your dog will learn to associate the presence of the stroller with controlled walking and you'll no longer need to use any verbal cues.

Practice this diligently in the weeks or even months before your child enters your life and going for a walk will present no problems when it's finally for real.

A Little Theater

The following exercise will require you to be a bit on the theatrical side. While seemingly silly, it's one more way to prepare both you and your dog for the very real changes that are heading your way.

Begin by buying a doll that is about the size of an actual baby. This is going to be your surrogate child until the real thing arrives and it will start to condition your dog to you carrying a bundle like this around. Additionally, it will enable you to teach him how to behave around this bundle. To complete your performance, see if you can acquire a blanket that already has the scent of a small infant on it. Often hospitals have used receiving blankets that they might be willing to part with. Otherwise, if you have a friend with a small child perhaps you could loan them a fresh blanket that they could use for a few days and then return to you fully scented. The

Photo: Rose Guilbert

idea, of course, is to swaddle the doll in this blanket and relate to it in front of your dog as if it were the genuine article.

Start carrying the faux baby around with you. While you might feel kind of silly doing so it will begin to give you a sense of the actuality of what you'll soon be dealing with. It will also allow you to get a sense of the most likely places that you might want to set your child down. Those are places that you should define zones around as described above. Additionally, *the "baby" itself should have a permanent zone around it.* Teaching this is quite simple, especially if you've already done everything outlined above. Whenever you set the "child" down, using your squirt bottle and an "out" command, teach your dog that he's not allowed near the "baby" without your permission. Of course, you should occasionally let him sniff the "baby" so that he can familiarize himself with the scent, and if you can do this only after asking him for a sit, so much the better. The idea, of course, is to teach the dog respect and propriety both in relation to the bundle in your hand as well as its scent.

Naturally, this implies that you don't do what some recent clients of mine mistakenly did, which is bring home the baby blanket and throw it on the floor. These folks thought that letting the dogs pee on and then tear up the blanket would be a great way to familiarize them with the scent. When their dogs bit their child in the face, predictably at the age of eight months, they were surprised, but they shouldn't have been. Teach your dog the right associations from early on.

GETTING CLOSER

As you approach your due date you will hopefully have dealt with any potential problem behaviors and have had a chance to implement a good deal of what's been discussed so far. Now you're in the home stretch and everything should be dovetailing nicely.

Getting All Dolled Up

Though seemingly silly, it's a good idea to get a baby doll, wrap it in a blanket, and teach your dog to treat it like he should the real thing. By doing so you can create a "template of behavior" which will help him to understand what's expected of him when the genuine article arrives.

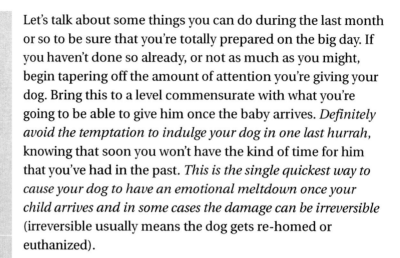

A Little Help Please

Dog walkers and other pet professionals are definitely people whose services you should consider enlisting. Their help can take enormous pressure off you and can often make the difference between a smooth transition and a disaster. Try and find a reputable person by asking around at your vet's and people at the local dog park. Satisfied customers are happy to share their experience and you want to find someone with lots of satisfied customers.

Let's talk about some things you can do during the last month or so to be sure that you're totally prepared on the big day. If you haven't done so already, or not as much as you might, begin tapering off the amount of attention you're giving your dog. Bring this to a level commensurate with what you're going to be able to give him once the baby arrives. *Definitely avoid the temptation to indulge your dog in one last hurrah,* knowing that soon you won't have the kind of time for him that you've had in the past. *This is the single quickest way to cause your dog to have an emotional meltdown once your child arrives and in some cases the damage can be irreversible* (irreversible usually means the dog gets re-homed or euthanized).

If you find that in the context of tapering your dog off his usual level of attention he is not getting the exercise that he needs, now might be the time to consider enlisting the services of a dog walker. A good dog walker will take your dog out with a group of other dogs to a safe, off-leash play area for an hour or so. There they will romp around, chase balls, wrestle, etc., and when he comes home he should be thoroughly exhausted. This will take the pressure off you as being the dog's primary source of entertainment. Doing this at least a month before your child arrives will ensure that your dog is comfortable with his walker and the dogs in his play group when the big day comes. In conjunction with this, it would also be a good idea to get your dog used to spending some time alone in the house in an isolated area such as a crate, behind a baby gate in the kitchen, the backyard or some other area where he does not have access to you. I promise you that there are going to be times when you simply want him out of your hair. A few daily periods of isolation should become a part of your dog's routine (If your dog has issues with separation anxiety see page 64). Of course, a special bone for him during these periods wouldn't hurt. And finally, it wouldn't be a bad idea to teach the dog to stay in a kennel or with a friend occasionally. If you haven't done so already, now would be a good time to introduce this as well. This will be particularly helpful on the day your child arrives, as you will see in a moment.

Photo: Rose Guilbert

As difficult as it is, you want to try to imagine what your life is going to look like once you have a child and condition your dog to that set of circumstances as soon as possible. If you really do this, the arrival of the baby will seem like a mere bump in the road in your dog's routine and he won't have the opportunity to build any negative associations with the addition of this new pack member. Beginning this work as long as possible before the baby's due date will mean that there'll be less for you to think about regarding your dog once the child is here. That's a good thing because frankly, once your child is here you're going to have precious few moments to think of anything other than the child. All that having been said, let's take a look at how to handle the big day and the months thereafter.

THE MOMENT OF TRUTH

With all the preparations made, you and your dog are now ready for the big event. As your due date becomes imminent you want to start thinking about what you're going to do with your dog while you're giving birth. My recommendation is to take advantage of the fact that he's been conditioned to boarding or staying with a friend periodically and put him there during this critical period. Even if your birth is of the "at home" variety, I would still recommend this. The birth process is notoriously unpredictable and knowing that your dog is in the good hands of someone else can give you at least a little peace of mind during this time. Your focus should be on the arrival of your child not on what's going on with your dog.

If you are not in a position to do this then I would be sure that the dog walker takes the dog out for an extra long outing the days surrounding the delivery, thus keeping him both busy and exhausted. This way, even if you're gone for an unusually long time, your dog will probably sleep right through it. If the dog walker option is also not a possibility for you then hopefully you will have conditioned the dog to tolerating occasionally long periods of time home alone. Whatever the case, you should now be in a position not to have to give your dog a second thought while your child is making his or her debut on Earth.

Once the debut is made, the time for introductions is at hand. If you have done your exercises with your dog and the baby doll (see page 104), your dog should have learned to gently sniff the little bundle with no jumping or pushy licking behaviors. Of course your dog is not stupid. He will immediately recognize that there is a universe of difference between that inanimate doll and the very much alive little child in your arms. However, he will have a "template of behavior" from his previous experience in a similar situation and most likely respond in the manner that you've taught him. Do not make a big deal out of the introduction. Be matter of fact about it and then go about your business.

When you put your child in his room or crib your dog should have learned his boundaries and naturally keep a respectful distance. If you'd like you may invite him into the area but it should always be in a very controlled manner. Since you've taught him to associate these areas with obedience commands previously he will expect to have to perform them now. Be sure to meet his expectations. Keep him in a sit-stay or a down-stay and don't forget to praise him when he complies. It's very easy to ignore good behavior and miss precious opportunities to positively reinforce the dog for behaviors you like.

Once your child is home and you're getting somewhat settled in, it might be a good time to put your dog in his special area so that he's just out of the way. Again, this is something that he will have learned and should have no trouble complying with. In fact, all of this should be so in line with what the dog has learned previously that, as I've said, the baby's arrival should be viewed as no big deal from the perspective of your dog.

Once initial introductions are out of the way you should simply continue with the routine you've established. Since your dog has been weaned off your attention he won't feel suddenly ostracized now. He'll expect to see his dog walker at midday, he'll be used to spending a part of the day alone in a special area, and he will have learned appropriate behaviors in relation to special zones in the house. The next step is to teach him to build very positive associations with the presence of your child.

In order to do this, I would suggest something that might initially seem somewhat counter-intuitive. More specifically, I recommend spending as much time with your dog in the presence of the child and significantly less time with him in the absence of the child. A great many people's inclinations would be to go and spend some time playing with the dog once the child is put up and to some degree there's no problem with that. By all means, if you want to play fetch or other very active games, do so once the child is taken care of. However, quiet moments of attention and affection should routinely take place in the presence of your child. Since you've been toning down your interactions with your dog in preparation for your child's arrival your attention will have become viewed as a valued resource from the perspective of the dog. By giving the dog access to this valued resource primarily in the presence of the child he will naturally view that presence as something very positive. Additionally, since you've taught him appropriate behaviors in relation to the

Making Friends

Once all the elements of control and propriety are in place you should work to develop as many positive associations for your dog with the presence of your child as possible. You want to be sure not to set up a competitive dynamic between the two of them, but build a close, cooperative and tolerant relationship between them instead. If you've followed the program thus far this should be as easy as changing diapers.

child's presence, these will be getting positively reinforced as well and thus continually strengthened. Let's take a look at what all this means in practical terms.

Say, for example, you're going to go into your child's room to play with him or perhaps just to do something functional such as change his diapers. At that point, invite your dog to join you in the room. Give him some attention in the form of a few quick obedience commands, reward him with a little loving and then ask him to do a down-stay. Attend to your child but here and there take a few moments out to verbally and, if possible, even physically praise your dog. An occasional treat wouldn't hurt either. Go back and forth between the two as seems appropriate to you at the moment. If, before this point, your dog has been relatively alone, he will definitely view this interaction in a positive light. If you're up for it, you can even fit junior into one of those Baby Bjorn™ type carriers where he's strapped onto your chest and then interact with your dog. The interaction can take the form of petting and stroking interspersed with some light obedience exercises. This will have the added benefit of beginning to teach your dog to associate your child with your authority and control. Be sure to add into this mix the handling exercises described on page 42 as well as the exercises around the food dish and objects of possession (see page 74) and this effect will be even further enhanced. The more you can do to teach your dog to associate your child with your authority, the better prepared you will be for the eight-month threshold when your child will become mobile, first by crawling then by walking. As stated above, it is usually here that real problems emerge between dogs and children if the appropriate preparatory steps have not been taken. Of course, if they have, then once again you should experience a seamless transition from one period to another.

The long and the short of it is that way too many people teach their dogs that when the baby is around, they're not. In other

Strap-Ons

Use the Baby Bjorn™ to your advantage by doing lots of handling and training exercises with your child thus attached. This will help your dog begin to associate your child with your power, authority and control – an attitude that will be very helpful once the little one begins to crawl.

words, the presence of the child means the absence of attention for the dog. Having prepared in the way I've described in the foregoing pages allows you to totally reverse this situation and teach your dog that the presence of the child means good things for him. In other words, any time that you spend with your child is an opportunity to build a bond not just between him and your dog but between all three of you.

Once your interaction time with your child is over, it's a good idea to make a point of terminating your interaction with your dog as well. Return him to his special place and go about your business. Again, this will serve to drive home the point that the child's presence means your presence and often its absence means yours as well. You don't want your dog viewing the child's absence as the beginning of his fun.

All this having been said there is one final rule that should be obeyed under any and every circumstance without exception and that is: *NO UNSUPERVISED INTERACTIONS BETWEEN YOUR DOG AND YOUR CHILD – EVER! NO EXCEPTIONS, PERIOD.* This is an absolute rule and should hold for years. It only takes a second for something to go wrong; but that second could change everyone's lives forever. Despite all the good training you've done, you should never take anything for granted because mistakes happen. Your dog could inadvertently knock your child over, he could be grabbing for a dog toy at the same time your child is and accidentally bite his hand. If you're not there, you'll never know exactly what happened. Who's going to pay the price? The dog, of course, since you now no longer trust him, a fact which can throw your whole relationship up in the air. If you are not in a position to supervise the interactions between the two, then separate them. That way you can be perfectly sure that nothing unfortunate will take place.

BAD NEWS

A recent newspaper article told the following story. A mother was working in the kitchen, about six feet away from her two-year-old daughter and six-year-old Rottweiler. She had taken her eyes off the two playmates for two seconds. During those two seconds the child spilled a bag of potato chips on the ground and then tried to pick them up. Since they'd fallen right at the dog's feet a confrontation developed and the dog severely bit the child causing life-threatening injuries which it will take many years and numerous surgeries to overcome. This dog had never shown a propensity toward violence previously and was by all accounts a nice dog. Unfortunately the mother made two mistakes: never teaching the dog about objects of possession and taking her eyes off the two of them for even two seconds. Never forget that it only takes two seconds for something to go horribly wrong.

As I've suggested above, the true test of whether all your work has been successful or not is the day your child becomes mobile, usually around eight months. It is at this point that the interactions between your dog and your child will become more frequent and unpredictable. Even with the best of supervision, the unexpected is guaranteed. It is likely, if you have been diligent in applying everything I've discussed so far, that there won't be any problems, however you should never be too bold in your assumptions. Don't make the mistake so many people make by letting down your guard. As your child evolves, the exercises you do with him and your dog should do so as well.

Continue to do handling exercises discussed on page 110 on a regular basis with your child in a Baby Bjorn™, or if he's getting too big, in your lap. Once he's old enough, have him begin to give simple obedience commands to your dog with you there to enforce them. You can begin by standing behind your child and actually moving his hands into the hand signals while both of you issue a simple command such as

Courtesy: Sharon Miner

"sit." If your dog refuses to comply, you gently but firmly demand compliance. If he does comply, let your child give him a treat (if he's capable – if not, then you reward). Again, move the child's hands in the appropriate manner if you need to. Continue to do this until your child is old enough to stand on his own in front of the dog and issue the commands. When you get to this point, you should try to fade out of the dog's awareness and get him to focus his attention on your child. The best way to accomplish this is to leash your dog and first, stand by his side, then later behind him. Your dog's focus should be on your child who should give the command and hand signal to the best of his ability. Again, if the dog complies he gets the treat from your child. If he does not you will enforce the command. Of course, by the time you've gotten to the point where you're able to stand behind the dog and have your child give direction he will have had so many exposures to this in increasing increments, that he really shouldn't have a problem. Continuing to do these exercises over the years as your child gets older is the best way to ensure that there'll never be a problem between them. Your dog will come to view your child as higher ranking and imbued with your authority.

A corollary to all of this, of course, is teaching your child how to be appropriate with your dog. It's unreasonable to expect your dog to tolerate endless harassment and torture from a young child who's incapable of appreciating the consequences of his actions. This is an important part of your child's education and will help him when he begins to encounter dogs other than yours. No matter how tolerant your dog is, you must teach your child not to kick, pull, pinch, poke or otherwise tease or torment the dog. You'll have to be very diligent here since most children are notoriously resistant to being scolded for such activity. Hence the admonition never to leave them unsupervised. Also teach your child never to suddenly jump on or surprise the dog while he's dead asleep or otherwise not aware of his presence. There's no telling how even the most well-behaved dog will respond when scared and startled. Teach your child to pet your dog in ways that are pleasurable and acceptable to your dog. If you've conditioned your dog to handle all kinds of rough

Behavior Boundaries Cut Both Ways

It's unreasonable to expect your dog to tolerate endless harassment and torture from a young child who's incapable of appreciating the consequences of his actions. This is an important part of your child's education and will help him when he begins to encounter dogs other than yours. No matter how tolerant your dog is, you must teach your child not to kick, pull, pinch, poke or otherwise tease or torment the dog.

handling using the exercises described on page 42 and you've taught your child how to handle your dog appropriately you've worked the problem from both ends and acquired the best insurance policy available against a bite.

As far as games are concerned, avoid having your child play strength or competitive games with your dog such as tug-of-war and chase. While they're okay for an adult who can initiate, control, and end the games (as described on page 41) it won't take your dog long to figure out that he's much quicker and stronger than your child. Once more, this is definitely information he can live without. You don't want to foster a physically confrontational and competitive atmosphere between your inter-species siblings. You want to cultivate a relationship based on mutual respect and self-control. The best games your child can play with your dog revolve around fetch, obedience exercises, and tricks. Tricks in particular are a great way to have the two of them interact. Most kids are thrilled to see their dog doing tricks and most dogs like doing them. They should be a source of lighthearted fun and entertainment for all concerned.

This brings us to one final point. If you've done everything right, your child and your dog will develop an extraordinary relationship with one another, the memory of which will be with your child forever. However, there is one potentially significant danger here. If your child lives with a very friendly and easygoing dog at home, he is naturally going to assume that every dog he encounters out in the world is equally as easygoing, an assumption that can lead to disaster. There are a great many dogs out and about that have no business mingling with the public at large. Trust me, I meet them all the time. If your child encounters one of these dogs and relates to him in the same way he's learned to relate to your dog at home, he can get himself seriously injured or worse. Therefore, it's extremely important to teach him from the earliest times how to relate to dogs he doesn't know.

Here are a few rules he should learn. First, your child should never approach a dog that is not accompanied by an adult. Second, he should never approach a dog without asking you first. Dogs that are tied out in front of a store waiting for their owners should be avoided at all costs. You know nothing about them and don't want to make any casual assumptions simply because it's a friendly looking Golden Retriever or something along those lines. If the dog is accompanied and you've given your child the okay, be sure to ask the adult whether or not the dog is friendly with children. *Never* let your child simply go up and pet the dog. If you sense any hesitation on the part of the adult, definitely pass. I continue to be amazed at the number of adults who simply ignore the hesitations or even outright warnings of dog owners when asked if their child can say hello and let their children approach the dog anyway. Such grossly irresponsible and cavalier behavior can lead to disaster. If the adult does give the okay, then have your child approach but observe a few rules about greeting strange dogs. Have the child approach the dog not face to face, but by offering his side to the side of the dog and holding out a closed hand for the dog to sniff. Do not allow him to approach the dog suddenly, rather teach him to approach slightly and let the dog make up the difference by coming towards him. If the dog is not interested nor showing any overt signs of friendliness, again please pass on the encounter. If he appears friendly and interested and approaches your child have your child pet him under the chin, not over the head, neck or back. The latter areas are considered "socially sensitive" and will cause some dogs to take offense. A stroke under the chin is much more acceptable. Direct face-to-face eye contact and hugs should be avoided at all costs.

Courtesy: Jane Reed

Finally, teach your child that if he sees a dog approaching, he should never run about and make loud shrieking sounds or strike at the dog, as children are prone to do. This common behavior can often put the dog in either a play or a prey mode, either of which can result in injuries to your child. If a dog approaches your child, whether slowly or fast, and whether friendly or not, teach your child to stand still, even if he's scared. If he thinks for some reason that the dog might bite him, teach him to put his clenched fists over his ears with his elbows coming down to his chest *and stand still*. The chances of any ill fortune befalling him under these circumstances are slim. Running around screaming and yelling dramatically increase the likelihood of something unpleasant occurring, as does striking out at the dog.

Following the few simple guidelines delineated above will help to ensure that your child's interactions with other people's dogs will always take place in a safe context and on a positive note.

Rules of Engagement

- *Never approach a dog unaccompanied by an adult.*
- *Never approach a dog without asking you first.*
- *Always ask the adult whether the dog is friendly.*
  - a) *If the adult seems uncomfortable, please pass on the interaction.*

- *If the adult gives the okay, have the child approach but observe a few rules:*
  - a) *Avoid face to face greetings.*
  - b) *Approach slightly and then have the dog make up the difference.*
  - c) *If the dog does not appear to be interested, please pass.*
  - d) *Have your child pet the dog under the chin, not over the head or back and please, no hugs.*

- *Do not run about wildly in the presence of a dog.*
  - a) *If you're concerned about the dog stand totally still and wait for him to lose interest or for someone to come and get him.*

In the foregoing pages I've covered quite a bit of material. While on the one hand it implies varying amounts of work, depending on your dog's behavior and disposition, on the other hand it promises a wholesome and fulfilling relationship between your child and your dog. The payoff of this relationship will last for years and thus makes any work you have to put in on the front end more than worth it. Therefore, I encourage you to make the effort to get it right.

If you find that you've followed the instructions in this book diligently but you're still having problems with your dog in relation to your child, there are two possibilities. The first is that you actually haven't done the work as diligently as you think and thus should consider revisiting it. The second is that possibly your dog is not ever going to be entirely reliable with your child. If the latter is the case, then I suggest re-homing the dog as soon as possible. No matter how well in control you might think you are, it's almost guaranteed that *if your dog is unreliable with your child sooner or later something unpleasant will happen.* It's really just a matter of time. Of course, in the end it's both the child and the dog that pay the price and therefore by finding the dog a more appropriate home now you're doing everyone a huge favor.

All that having been said, I wish you the best of luck with the exciting events that are unfolding in your life. Few things provide a living connection to the mystery of what it means to be alive like the opportunity to be the vehicle for a new life entering this world. The struggles that are involved in

One big, happy family!

nurturing this new being and orienting it to its existence in this world pale by comparison to the joy of watching that little being unfold itself. The fact that we participate in this mystery is in itself extraordinary and should be the source of the deepest joy. Providing a wonderful home for a dog, that most loyal and devoted of animal companions, in this context should only enrich this experience. With this in mind I leave you with best wishes and heartfelt blessings.

Courtesy: Jane Reed

APPENDIX

PINCH COLLARS VS. CHOKE CHAINS

Two of the fundamental instruments of control with which most people are familiar these days are pinch collars and choke chains. In my view, there is a great deal of confusion about these two items. Generally speaking, most people view the pinch collar, based on its appearance, as an inherently vicious device while they view the choke chain as something that, while perhaps marginally unpleasant, is necessary and not particularly abusive. After all, choke chains have been used for years by all sorts of renowned trainers and our dogs don't seem to be any worse off for it. On the other hand, one look at a pinch collar and the first impression most people get is that of a 12th century torture device and their first response is "not on my dog." In fact, I myself held the same view until I took a closer look at the whole issue.

Let's quickly examine the mechanics of these two instruments beginning with the choke chain. The choke chain is a rather harmless looking device, a simple piece of chain with a ring on either side. This is placed around the dog's neck in such a way that if you snap the chain, it constricts around the soft tissue of the neck. This means that the chain becomes a band of steel putting pressure on the dog's muscles, arteries, and trachea all the way around his neck. In other words, you're potentially bruising your dog, cutting off blood flow to his brain, and restricting his flow of oxygen, clearly not a healthy situation. Moreover, because the choke chain is relatively unaversive from the perspective of your dog, you often have to deliver a substantial correction in order to be able to modify his behavior. Clearly, the harder the correction you have to deliver, the more pressure you are exerting on all the soft tissue I just mentioned. Again, this is not a healthy situation despite the relatively innocuous appearance of the choke chain.

The pinch collar, on the other hand, operates on completely different principles. The most important thing about the pinch collar is *what it does not do*. It does not put a band of steel around your dog's neck and constrict all the soft tissue in that area every time a correction is delivered. In fact, the purpose of the pinch collar is to eliminate this type of potentially damaging impact on your dog's neck altogether. Taking a closer look at the pinch collar we start by examining the prongs on the links that make up the collar. A close examination will reveal that the prongs themselves are dull and rounded, and not sharp at all. The point of the collar (no pun intended) is not to puncture the dog, it is to pinch muscle and fur, a momentarily unpleasant but entirely harmless sensation. In other words, no matter how hard a correction you have to give the dog, there is never a band of steel around his neck nor the concomitant pressure on the soft tissue. Moreover, the sensation of a pinch collar correction is *immediately* more aversive than that of a choke chain correction, meaning that a fraction of the force is required in order to get a response from the dog. In fact, *the net result of using a pinch collar for corrections is the reduction of force on your dog by about 95 percent and the elimination of any possibility of injuring the dog* when properly used. What might require a two-fisted correction with a choke chain can usually be accomplished with a flick of the wrist on a pinch collar. Finally, training the dog to recognize and respect the pinch collar is usually a matter of less than five minutes, which is why many trainers, myself included, refer to it as power steering for dogs.

There some other factors to consider. Most dogs have an organic reference point for understanding what a pinch collar correction is all about. In other words, when a dog reprimands another dog it's often with a quick bite on the neck, which, of course, would result in a pinching sensation. This is something that they have learned from their earliest days in the litter both from Mom and their littermates. On the other hand, a dog has no organic reference point for a choking sensation, potentially making its interpretation more difficult. The long and short of it is that in this case appearances are deceiving. While the pinch collar looks like a fairly vicious and potentially damaging training device and the choke chain appears relatively harmless, the reverse is actually the case. It is for this reason that I prefer to use pinch collars (where corrections are required) and I never use choke chains.

If you are planning to use a pinch collar with your dog, be sure that you fit the collar snugly. The contact points should be practically standing up on the dog's neck. Many people believe they are doing their dog a favor by putting the collar on loosely but the reverse is actually the case. First of all, the looser the pinch collar is fitted the harder you have to pull in order for the collar to have its effect. Secondly, if the collar is too loose, rather than pinching as it's supposed to do when a nudge is delivered, it's possible to actually drive the prongs into the dog's neck. This is definitely not the collar's purpose. Finally, if the collar is on too loose it's possible for another dog to get his mouth or even entire head trapped under the collar potentially leading to disastrous consequences. Related to this, please be aware that the pinch collar should only be on the dog when the leash is on him. He should never be allowed to play with other dogs with the pinch collar on and by the same token you should never allow your dog to play with another dog that has a pinch collar on.

NOTES